The Philosophy of Education of William Torrey Harris in the Annual Reports

Peter M. Collins

UNIVERSITY PRESS OF AMERICA,® INC.
Lanham • Boulder • New York • Toronto • Plymouth, UK

Copyright © 2008 by
University Press of America,® Inc.
4501 Forbes Boulevard
Suite 200
Lanham, Maryland 20706
UPA Acquisitions Department (301) 459-3366

Estover Road
Plymouth PL6 7PY
United Kingdom

All rights reserved
Printed in the United States of America
British Library Cataloging in Publication Information Available

Library of Congress Control Number:
ISBN-13: 978-0-7618-3991-0 (paperback : alk. paper)
ISBN-10: 0-7618-3991-7 (paperback : alk. paper)

∞™ The paper used in this publication meets the minimum
requirements of American National Standard for Information
Sciences—Permanence of Paper for Printed Library Materials,
ANSI Z39.48—1984

This book is dedicated to my lovely and loving wife,
Mary Ann Lee Collins,
who always will be Pei Tzu Li.

Contents

Preface	vii
Acknowledgments	xi
1 Background and Nature of the Topic	1
Harris and the Annual Reports	1
The Annual Reports: Commentaries from Selected Secondary Sources	3
2 Philosophy of Education in the Annual Reports	9
Preliminary Remarks	9
Observations about Philosophy of Education	9
Examples of Philosophy of Education	11
Introductory Commentary	11
General Nature of the Human Person and Education	12
The Human Mind and Education	15
Human Socialization and Education	20
Human Freedom and Education	26
Morality (and Religion) and Education	30
Religion and Education	36
Summary	37
3 Summary and Conclusion	47
4 Epilogue	53
Bibliography	55
About the Author	59

Preface

The three intertwining careers of William Torrey Harris (1835–1909) (in philosophy, philosophy of education, and educational administration) converge in twelve of the Annual Reports of the Board of Directors of the St. Louis Public Schools. Most of the essential features of these twelve reports Harris formulated as the Superintendent of Schools from 1867 to 1879. These particular Reports, which have been acclaimed nationally and internationally, and are said to be among the most valuable official publications in American educational literature, are far different from the descriptive documents originally intended by their author.

The major purpose of this study is to demonstrate that Harris, as Superintendent of the St. Louis Public Schools, provided in his Annual Reports an authentic philosophy of education in the sense of explanations of interrelated philosophical principles and their applications to educational problems. An attempt is made to show that Harris not only writes about philosophy of education (stressing its importance) in these documents, but also that he does philosophy of education in them.

The substance of the examples of Harris's philosophy of education which are analyzed in this paper is focused upon a broadly based philosophical anthropology (or philosophy of the person) in relationship primarily to the purposes, curriculum, and teaching methods in intellectual, moral, and religious education. The first category of examples centers upon Harris's philosophy of the person, in general, and its implications for education; while the next five sections are classified according to key philosophical attributes of the person: mindfulness, socialization, freedom, morality, and religiousness. These five characteristics are featured (in order) in Harris's philosophical psychology and epistemology, social and political philosophy, philosophy of freedom, moral philosophy, and philosophy of religion. In each section, I relate the philosophical principles to educational topics by means of two or more examples. (Harris himself rarely depicts this relationship explicitly.)

The importance of the interrelationships and the unity of these six categories scarcely can be overemphasized in any attempt to appreciate Harris's philosophy of education in his Annual Reports. General features include the dualistic conception of the person and the consequent educational purposes characterizing the general spirit of the philosophy of education which emerges from the six categories of examples. The dualistic conception of the human being is based upon the fundamental distinction between matter and spirit, which is humanly manifested by the body and soul. The powers of the soul consist of the intellect (for knowing) and the will (for choosing). This material-spiritual being called the person also can be viewed as individual-social; only through socialization, or physical and immaterial combination with others, can the person become more human in relationship with God. Within this dualistic framework, immaterial being is afforded a primacy which is extremely significant for the purposes of education.

Educators, in implementing the development of the person, must take serious account of this dualistic structure of reality. The purposes of education include developing the body and the soul, including the intellect and the will, in a manner conducive to material and spiritual combination with others, which renders human beings truly free. In all cases, the physical growth is intended generally to serve and to promote spiritual maturation. The latter, when attached to the intellect, is intellectual education; when associated with the will, it is moral education; and when it is directed to the union of the person with the Divine, it is religious education. Intellectual education is established upon a curriculum with five subjects of study, which are gradually expanded as the student enters the higher levels of the process. Moral education is undertaken with a basic intent to discipline the student in order to promote an attitude of self-sacrifice. Religious education is the highest form of all and is to be conducted under the auspices of the church.

It becomes evident upon further analysis that the philosophical principles proposed by Harris are consistent with—and, in fact, apparently inspired—the pattern of education recommended. A basic example of this consistency lies in the parallel between different modes of immaterial being (intellect, will, and God) and different kinds of education (intellectual, moral, and religious).

While the primary sources utilized in this study were intended officially to be descriptions of the process of education (in the St. Louis Public Schools), it is evident that William Torrey Harris produced in them a network of philosophical principles elaborated as a foundation for his educational theory. This fact, in historical perspective, suggests the need for further related research, not the least significant of which pertains to the relationship of Harris's philosophy of education to the American cultural revolution (from approximately 1880 to 1920), to its early aftermath, and to the contemporary analytic movement in American philosophy of education.

Acknowledgments

Since the initial preparation for completing this book goes back several years, I am indebted to too many former colleagues to mention them all by name. I hope that they will accept this expression of my gratitude. However, a few debts call for specific mention. These include Dr. Adrian Dupuis, who accepted me as a new faculty colleague in philosophy of education at Marquette University, Milwaukee, WI, many years ago and was so generous in promoting my professional development. I also owe a debt of gratitude to my former colleague, the late Dr. Robert Nordberg and to his wife, Dr. Beverly Nordberg, whose friendship I still cherish. Bob Nordberg always evaluated my work—and myself—at levels which I never could have expected to attain.

I would like to mention three others, who were called away early: one a former colleague at Marquette, Dr. Wasyl (Bill) Shimoniak; and two who were not only tennis friends, but also very good friends, John Duckworth and Perry Raines. I also am grateful to the late Rev. John Campbell, S.J., of Gesu Church in Milwaukee and to the late Rev. Auguste Lespade, M.P., a French missionary in Taiwan, who were vital instruments of God's goodness in my life.

I was fortunate to be associated in those days at Marquette with Ms. Doris Kirchberg, an administrative assistant and error-free typist. She also was one of my outstanding graduate students—who, I fear, still has not forgiven me for losing her personal statement of philosophy of education, which was a class requirement! My thanks must be extended also to another administrative assistant who typed most of the final draft of this book, Ms. Joanne Devlin of the Department of Philosophy at Saint Joseph's University in Philadelphia, who convinced me—as she does everyone—that "The Hawk Will Never Die!"

My gratitude at the institutional level is owed to the Graduate School of Marquette University, Milwaukee, WI, for a Summer Faculty Fellowship and other research grants which supported research for this project. I am grateful also for the patient and timely assistance of Ms. Patti Belcher of University Press of America; her guidance in the publication process was essential. Finally, no terrestrial being deserves more credit for anything that I have accomplished since 1999 (the year in which we were married on the feast of St. Ignatius Loyola) than my wife Mary Ann Lee Collins, to whom this book is dedicated.

Chapter One

Background and Nature of the Topic

HARRIS AND THE ANNUAL REPORTS

The three intertwining careers of William Torrey Harris (1835–1909), (in philosophy, philosophy of education, and educational administration) converged in twelve of the Annual Reports of the Board of Directors of the St. Louis Public Schools. Most of the essential features of .these twelve reports Harris formulated as the Superintendent of Schools from 1867 to 1879.[1] His philosophical career is associated typically with the St. Louis Philosophical Movement (particularly the efforts of the St. Louis Philosophical Society, which he founded in 1866), the *Journal of Speculative Philosophy* (which he founded and edited from 1867 to 1893), and the Concord School of Philosophy (1880–1889). His educational career is linked most prominently with his work as Superintendent of the St. Louis Public Schools (1867–1880)[2] and United States Commissioner of Education in Washington, D.C. (1889–1906).[3]

While Harris's historical importance and fame are attested in numerous volumes,[4] the following comment also signals the fact of his three integrated careers: "His contributions to philosophy and to the theory and practice of education were not only numerous, but of commanding importance. The history of American education and of our American contributions to philosophical thought cannot be understood or estimated without knowledge of the life work of Dr. William Torrey Harris."[5] Furthermore, he has been referred to as "America's first great educational philosopher."[6]While this assertion raises some questions, perhaps a modified version of it could be justified. Kilpatrick offers a more specific comment in this regard: "It seems rather probable that the translation of Rosenkranz made under Dr. Harris' direction gave the term 'philosophy of education' its first strong hold in America."[7]

The Annual Reports of the Board of Directors of the St. Louis Public Schools for which Harris was responsible are not always viewed as treatises in philosophy of education in the sense of embodying explicated philosophical principles applied to educational problems. However, the following analysis of the pertinent documents is intended to demonstrate that, in formulating these Reports, Harris the educational administrator was engaged in directly philosophical activity employed in relationship to the consideration of various educational questions or topics. That is, one can locate in portions of these Annual Reports written by Harris distinctly philosophical principles, expressly educational principles, and explicit as well as implicit relationships between the two categories.

Evidence for the fact that this kind of report was not intended originally by Harris is found in his citation of his predecessor (Divoll) concerning the purpose of these annual publications:

> I am called upon, not to discuss new theories and principles, not to write elaborate essays on the subjects of education, but to make such a statement of facts as will enable your constituents, the citizens of St. Louis, who bear the expense and enjoy the benefits of the Public Schools, to judge correctly of their management, their present position, their progress, and their future prospects.[8]

On the other hand, there are some bases for appreciating Harris's inclination to produce the kind of school reports which he did: his own philosophical abilities and interests; and the practical orientation of the St. Louis Philosophical Society, of which he was a leader. According to one commentator, "the members of the Philosophical Society felt that philosophy had a public service to perform . . . its function [was] to make clear the great thoughts that help us to live."[9] Furthermore, education was a prime area of concern for the practical application of philosophy in this group: "The dominant and rather astonishing characteristic of this St. Louis movement of thought was that it centered around the public schools. . . . The St. Louis group was mostly teachers in the city schools."[10] Therefore, it appears that, with some detailed elaboration, one might be successful in defending the contention that these Annual Reports of Harris are documents integral to the St. Louis Philosophical Movement and strongly indicative of its tenor.

The major purpose of this study is to demonstrate that Harris, as Superintendent of the St. Louis Public Schools, provided an authentic philosophy of education in his Annual Reports. This purpose is pursued by two integrally related means: 1) clarifying the fundamental philosophical and educational principles as found in these Reports, and 2) explaining relationships between the selected philosophical and educational principles. Upon the demonstrability of the central thesis rests the possibility of illustrating herein a fundamental meaning of "philosophy of education" prominent in the American heritage.

An observer might question what, if any, reasons exist for engaging in this investigation in light of the fact that Harris provided an explicit statement of his philosophy of education in a book entitled *Psychologic Foundations of Education* (1898).[11] Truly, there is a potential problem of redundancy, especially in light of a commentator's insistence that Harris' thought never developed substantially after his St. Louis period.[12] However, there are several factors to consider in response to this concern. First, his Annual Reports apparently have not been analyzed in the precise manner undertaken here. Secondly, this mode of approach appears important, if not necessary, in clarifying the meanings of the Report themselves and in rendering an explicit comparison of the Annual Reports with the *Psychologic Foundations of Education*. Thirdly, one would expect to find some difference, at least in tone, between these two important sources of his thought in light of the enhanced polemical character of Harris's circumstances by 1898, the year of publication of this book. Fourthly, even if no "development" of thought would be discovered in a minutely detailed comparison of the two sources, that would be some evidence for the conclusion that Harris's principles exposed in the Annual Reports represent not only the "bedrock" of the *Psychologic Foundations*, but also his most mature thought in this area (presuming that there were no substantial shifts in his thought after 1898). Finally, the historical importance of these Annual Reports, in light of the apparent fact that they have not been subjected to this kind of scrutiny, warrants such an investigation as that proposed.[13]

Before adverting directly to the primary sources in attempting to justify and explain the stated thesis, attention is turned to selected comments of various observers concerning Harris's Annual Reports. The main purpose of this next section is to supply some general information concerning the nature and context of these Annual Reports as a further basis for appreciating the details to follow.

THE ANNUAL REPORTS: COMMENTARIES FROM SELECTED SECONDARY SOURCES

The remarks of these commentators will be considered in three categories: an introduction to the Annual Reports of the Board of Directors of the St. Louis Public Schools, the influence or importance of them, and a conclusion. Among the introductory items is one concerning the initiation of Harris's efforts in formulating the basic features of the Annual Reports. Although Assistant Superintendent Harris had labored intensely on the Thirteenth Annual Report,[14] it appeared over Superintendent Divoll's signature. However, Harris did assume full responsibility for the Fourteenth Annual Report for the year ending August 1, 1868, having become the Superintendent in 1867. (This report was published in 1869, the year following the academic year to which it referred, establishing a precedent for dating the Annual Reports.)[15]

Further introduction to the Annual Reports through these selected secondary sources concerns the purposes of them and some effects, their general tenor, and their timeliness. Kohlbrenner notes three purposes of the Annual Reports: 1) to familiarize the members of the School Board and St. Louis citizens with the condition of the schools, 2) to educate this audience in the principles and practices of education, and 3) to popularize the efforts and achievements of the local schools beyond the immediate community.[16] A similar consideration in another source, although viewed in terms of accomplished fact, yields three distinct effects of Harris's Annual Reports: they 1) provided an account of school activities and costs, 2) promoted the taxpayers to take pride in their schools as partners in establishing "the finest Public School system," and 3) inculcated in the citizens of St. Louis an awareness that they were contributing to the development of American democracy and humanity by supporting the schools.[17]

As noted above, Harris's Annual Reports were comprised not merely of statistical data and other facts, but also of theoretical discussions of prominent educational questions. They were "a distinct departure from the run of dry compilations of mummified pedagogues," according to Harris's main biographer.[18] The substance of these reports was not dictated by the rules of the School Board,[19] which suggests the possibility of a great deal of freedom and initiative on the part of Harris in their formulation. The numerous topics he included were chosen on one or more of several criteria (not all mutually exclusive): the form and arrangement of these reports developed by his predecessors, state law, information required by the nature of the circumstances, typical content of such documents, his own special interests, general interest within and beyond the boundaries of the city, local and general controversy, and local and general demand for new development.[20]

The second of the three topics focusing upon background from the secondary sources concerns the influence or importance of the Annual Reports. One noted American educator (in 1900) ranked them among the most valuable official publications in American educational literature (along with the school reports of Horace Mann as Secretary of the State Board of Education of Massachusetts [1838–49], and the annual reports of Charles W. Eliot as President of Harvard University [1871–99]).[21] These Annual Reports of the Board of Directors of the St. Louis Public Schools for which Harris was largely responsible have been touted virtually as educational classics.[22] According to Leidecker, even Harris's philosophical-pedagogical contribution to the Thirteenth Annual Report (published under Divoll's name) received complimentary remarks from all the reviewers.[23]

The scope of the influence achieved through these annual publications during the Harris superintendency appears to be extraordinary. In a published account of the St. Louis Movement, Snider recollects that "by his [Harris's] annual reports as well as by his addresses he made an epoch in education, not only locally but throughout the nation."[24] His Annual Reports became models for other superintendents in the United States, and ". . . they were read and quoted nationally and internationally."[25] Kohlbrenner asserts that by means of the Annual Reports "national and even international recognition was given to him [Harris] personally and to the St. Louis schools."[26] Several instances of national recognition between 1873 and 1875 are specified.[27] Leidecker refers to the uncommonly abundant correspondence of Harris brought about by discussions evoked by the reports throughout this country and in Europe, especially in Germany.[28] Further evidence of the international fame of Harris and the St. Louis Public Schools lies in their association with the Vienna Exposition of 1873 and the Paris Universal Exposition of 1878. Both Harris and St. Louis were awarded honors through the latter, and the Annual Reports of Harris were subsequently placed in the Pedagogical Library being organized in the Palais Bourbon.[29]

Reasons mentioned for such widespread attention to the Annual Reports, in addition to the quality of the education which they described, are Harris's appealing literary style,[30] the timeliness of the topics, and the "thorough and decisive manner in which Harris stated his views."[31] At least two commentators emphasize the existence of philosophy of education in these Annual Reports;[32] without accepting or rejecting the authority of these observers, it is intended in the remainder of this paper to provide evidence for the meaning of their assertions.

NOTES

1. The Annual Reports referred to include the Fourteenth (published in 1869) through the Twenty-fifth (published in 1880). Although Harris, as Assistant Superintendent, "had worked vigorously" on the Thirteenth Annual Report, it appeared over the signature of Superintendent Ira Divoll. The Fourteenth Annual Report (for the year ending August 1, 1868) was the first one for which Harris assumed complete responsibility. See Kurt F. Leidecker, *Yankee Teacher: The Life of William Torrey Harris* (New York: The Philosophical Library, 1946,; New York: Kraus Reprint Company, 1971), 183.

2. Harris was also Superintendent of the Concord (Massachusetts) Public Schools, from 1882 to 1885, although that fact seems to have escaped notice in practically all of the pertinent secondary sources. See Leidecker, *Yankee Teacher*, 428–30. Leidecker refers to Harris's service in this capacity as "completely forgotten," 429.

3. Leidecker's *Yankee Teacher*, while not uncriticized, is the most complete single source of information concerning the life and work of Harris.

4. Investigations related to this study have turned up many secondary sources iterating the prominence or influence of one or more aspects of Harris's undertakings. Perhaps, his founding of the *Journal of Speculative Philosophy* in 1867 (the first philosophical journal in the country), and the founding of the kindergarten under his leadership in the St. Louis Public Schools in 1873 (the first kindergarten in the United States under public school auspices) are the most frequently mentioned of his contributions in philosophy and in education, respectively. Ford claims that Harris's Annual Report to the St. Louis Public School Directors for 1871 "was the first to give system to concrete education . . . a great step towards articulating the public school system from the kindergarten to the university." See T.B. Ford, "William Torrey Harris: an Educational Reformer," *Studies in Honor of William Torrey Harris*, *International Education Review* (Berlin: Weidmannsche Buchhandklung, (1935), 250. (The entire article covers 242–250.) In the same volume see Lucy M. Schwiener, "William Torrey Harris, Influence of His St. Louis Period," 554–60; and John S. Roberts, "Educational Contributions of William Torrey Harris," 237–42.

5. Nicholas Murray Butler, "Foreword," Leidecker, *Yankee Teacher,* v. Another passage which seems to connote a similar notion is the first paragraph of Merle Curti's "William T. Harris, The Conservator," in his book *The Social Ideas of American Educators*, with New Chapter on the Last Twenty-five Years, New and revised edition (Totowa, NJ: Littlefield, Adams, 1966), 310. However, while Curti's work has been held in high esteem, it might be contended that his theme in this article (which is expressed in the passage referred to) appears to be seriously short-sighted from a religious-theological-philosophical-educational perspective: while Harris's efforts might have had the appearance of "conservation" for a very limited time, his philosophy of religion seems to have opened the floodgates in the "watershed" of American intellectual history, including both philosophy and educational theory. (For the use and meaning of "watershed" in this context, see Henry Steele Commager, *The American Mind: An Interpretation of American Thought and Character Since the 1800's* [New Haven: Yale University Press, 1956], Chapter II, 41–54.)

6. Paul Monroe (ed.), *The Cyclopedia of Education*, Vol. III (New York: The Macmillan Company, 1911–1913), 220. This phrase is cited by William H. Kilpatrick, "Tendencies in Educational Philosophy," *Twenty-five Years of American Education, Collected Essays*, Ed. I.L. Kandel (New York: The Macmillan Company, 1929), 61.

7. Ibid. The "translation of Rosenkranz. . . ." refers to Johann Karl Friedrich Rosenkranz, *The Philosophy of Education*, International Education Series, Tr. Anna C. Brackett (New York: D. Appleton & Company, 1886). Harris edited a large number of volumes in Appleton's International Education Series, the first of which was this book by the Hegelian Rosenkranz.

8. Fourteenth Annual Report of the Board of Directors of the St. Louis Public Schools for the Year Ending August 1, 1868 (St. Louis: George Knapp and Company, Printers and Binders, 1869), Kohlbrenner cites this passage and then comments, "Therewith Harris proceeded to discuss the course of study for the St. Louis schools by launching into a comparison of the characteristic differences in Oriental and Occidental civilization. This procedure was more or less typical of the attitude he assumed toward his reports. While he did not often fail to include the required prosaic statistical data he evidenced a desire to go beyond the factual part of the summary and to delve into theoretical questions. His reports were, therefore, not merely official papers required by his position but a series of essays on the most discussed educational topics of the time." Bernard J. Kohlbrenner, "William Torrey Harris, Superintendent of Schools, St. Louis, Missouri, 1868–1880," Unpublished doctoral dissertation, Graduate School of Education, Harvard University, 1950.

9. Charles E. Witter, "The St. Louis Philosophical Movement and the St. Louis Public Schools," *School and Society*, 47 (March 26, 1938), 404.

10. Ibid. The practice-oriented philosophical interests of the St. Louis philosophers of this era also are pointed out in other secondary sources.

11. William Torrey Harris, *Psychologic Foundations of Education: An Attempt to Show the Genesis of the Higher Faculties of Mind*, International Education Series, Vol.37 (New York: D. Appleton & Company. 1898). It should be mentioned that the title of the book refers to the clarification of principles of (primarily) philosophical psychology applied to educational matters. Harris staunchly resisted efforts to associate psychology exclusively with empirical procedures.

12. Snider refers to the years 1865–80 as Harris' "highest creative period." Denton J. Snider, *The St. Louis Movement in Philosophy, Literature, Education, Psychology*, with Chapters of Autobiography (St. Louis: Sigma Publishing Company, 1920).

13. Roberts' book on Harris's philosophy of education appears to be the only book-length study of its kind. However, this was published in 1924 and is directed only to an analysis of his writings published after 1880. John Stacy Roberts, *William Torrey Harris: A Critical Study of His Educational and Related Philosophical Views* (Washington, DC: National Education Association of the United States, 1924).

14. Thirteenth Annual Report of the Board of Directors of the St. Louis Public Schools for the Year Ending August 1, 1867 (St. Louis: Missouri Democrat Book and Job Printing House, 1867). In addition to whatever unofficially recognized contributions Harris made to this volume, he also formulated the "Report of the Assistant Superintendent" (56–73).

15. Leidecker, 183.

16. Kohlbrenner, 60.

17. Leidecker, 256–57.

18. Ibid., 256.

19. Kohlbrenner, 61.

20. Ibid., 61–62.

21. Nicholas Murray Butler, "Introduction," *Education in the United States, A Series of Monographs*, Ed. Nicholas Murray Butler, Vol. I (Albany, NY: J.B. Lyon, 1900), xvii.

22. For notices of other commendations of these reports, the reader can consult Leidecker, 257, 373, 376–77; Kohlbrenner, 62; Payson Smith, "In Appreciation of William T. Harris," *William Torrey Harris: The Commemoration of the One Hundredth Anniversary of His Birth, 1835–1935*, Ed. Walton C. John, Bulletin 1936, No. 17, Office of Education, U.S. Department of the Interior (Washington, DC: U.S. Government Printing Office, 1937), 14; and Ernest Sutherland Bates, *"Harris, William Torrey,"* Dictionary of American Biography (Under the Auspices of the American Council of Learned Societies), Ed. Dumas Malone, Vol. VIII (New York: Charles Scribners Sons, 1932), 328–30.

23. Leidecker, 183.

24. Snider, 96.

25. Ford, "William Torrey Harris: An Educational Reformer," *Studies in Honor of William Torrey Harris, International Education Review*, 248.

26. Kohlbrenner, 62.

27. Ibid., 62–63.

28. Leidecker, 257.

29. Ibid., 373, 376–77. For Harris's honors in France, see also "Harris, William Torrey," *Encyclopedia of the History of Missouri: A Compendium of History and Biography for Ready Reference*, Ed. Howard L. Conard, Vol. 3 (New York: The Southern History Company; Haldeman, Conard and Company, Proprietors, 1901), 190–201.

30. Ford, "William Torrey Harris: An Educational Reformer," *Studies in Honor of William Torrey Harris, International Education Review*, 248.

31. Kohlbrenner, 62–63.

32. Kohlbrenner, 64; and Smith, "In Appreciation of William T. Harris," *William Torrey Harris: The Commemoration of the One Hundredth Anniversary of His Birth, 1835–1935,*" 14.

Chapter Two

Philosophy of Education in the Annual Reports

PRELIMINARY REMARKS

Some indication of the importance of philosophy of education to Harris in his Annual Reports is found in his remarks *about* that discipline. These remarks concern primarily a need for philosophy of education. However, the central feature of the evidence to support the thesis of this paper is found in the examples of philosophy of education provided by Harris in those Reports. For the most part, each example is extracted from a single passage (extending over approximately one to five pages). Although parts of the same general content may be employed more than once, the use of a particular passage is not repeated.[1]

OBSERVATIONS ABOUT PHILOSOPHY OF EDUCATION

In commenting in his Annual Reports upon the need for philosophy of education, Harris is direct and explicit. In two instances he complains about the lack of attention to psychology of education; "psychology" signifies to him principles of philosophical psychology, or the philosophy of mind or of mental operations.[2] First, he expresses a desire "to call the attention of educators to certain problems in psychology which concern very closely the methods employed in the school-room."[3] He is referring to "learning problems" of students, which provoke the need for study and discussion by teachers. He laments the lack of a journal "in which Psychology is discussed in its relations to Pedagogy."[4] Commenting on the difficulties of student learning in relationship to the curriculum, he claims that "It is owing to the lack of psychological insight that we have so many changes in theories and systems, so much advocacy of one-sided extremes. Caprice and arbitrariness determine the choice of this or that study. The likes and dislikes of the teacher settle the course of the pupil; the whim of the parent is allowed to do the same thing."[5]

In another place there is an emphasis on the need for those "who have the direction of education" (as teachers and "supervisors of schools") to study the history of education. However, the names (Darwin, Plato, Aristotle, Comte, and Spencer) and some principles mentioned (as the Platonic dialectic and the doctrine of teleology or final causes) suggest that what is intended is the history of philosophy of education. Harris refers to his own philosophical stance in saying that "If idealism has any truth—if there is any basis for a spiritual theory of the universe—it will become manifest to us in a study of the history of the world and of mankind. Educational thinkers, above all others must be active in this field, and see to it that no merely preliminary and half-views be forced upon them."[6]

Other specific individuals also are linked to comments promoting the study of philosophy of education. Apparently with reference to Pestalozzi's choices in establishing a curriculum, Harris asserts that philosophy, not merely empirical inquiry (object-lessons for Pestalozzi), is needed to ascertain the most valuable of a number of objects. In regard to this problem of life and of education, Pestalozzi "needed a system of Philosophy to give him the comprehensive views required for classification, and hence could arrive at nothing fixed, or free from self-contradiction."[7] Froebel is brought into a similar kind of discussion at least twice. He is said to have "carefully considered the order of evolution of the faculties of the mind" before establishing a curriculum.[8] Considering Froebel's educational theory again, Harris advises the reader to note the importance of "settling" questions in psychology in order to appreciate fully the plan of Froebel. According to Harris, "There are deeper grounds than merely national ones. . . . There is human nature in general and the law of its unfolding—common to all civilized nations."[9] In the context of Harris' thought, these are direct references to philosophy of education.

In conclusion to these remarks of Harris about philosophy of education, it is evident that this discipline is important to him and that he sees it as a vital dimension of every professional educator's awareness. In fact, Harris claims that in philosophy of religion[10] one discovers the most important feature of the person, namely, the nature of his final destiny. Without knowledge of this destiny, the educator cannot identify a direction for the process of education and, therefore, fails necessarily to provide any intelligible means of education.

> The close relation of morality, which includes special duties, to religion, which contains the ultimate and supreme ground of all obligations, has led to the con-

nection which we see everywhere existing between the system of education and the national religion. The national religion in defining its relation to God, defines its idea of the final destiny of man. Not only does education, moral and intellectual, depend directly upon this, but the form of government, the constitution of civil society, likewise presuppose that basis.[11]

Without minimizing the pertinence and weightiness of these comments of Harris about philosophy of education, they obviously do little to specify the details of his own philosophy of education as found in his Annual Reports. Most of the remainder of this book is addressed to that matter.

EXAMPLES OF PHILOSOPHY OF EDUCATION

Introductory Commentary

The following examples of Harris's philosophy of education in his Annual Reports could be categorized in various manners. However, the general substance lends itself to a focus on the nature of the person (philosophical anthropology) and educational implications. The following specific topics will be considered in the order listed: 1) nature of the human person, in general, and education, 2) the human mind and education, 3) human socialization and education, 4) human freedom and education, 5) morality (and religion) and education, and 6) religion and education. The corresponding areas of philosophy of most direct concern in the last five topics are 2) philosophical psychology and epistemology, 3) social and political philosophy, 4) philosophy of freedom, 5) moral philosophy, and 6) philosophy of religion.

The specific educational issues scrutinized here will vary from section to section depending upon the texts. However, the three most prominent are the typical ones: purposes (also called goals, aims, ends, or objectives) of education, curriculum, and teaching methods. These three dimensions of the process are suggested respectively by the following questions: Why should education be undertaken? What should be taught? How should one teach? Related matters of direct concern to Harris the educator are agencies of education, the school library, and evening school. The importance of the interrelationships among these topics must be emphasized, of course.

In explaining the relationships between the philosophical principles and the educational recommendations according to Harris in his Annual Reports, one could initiate the discussion on either side. Beginning with education and inquiring into the philosophical foundations of the educational theory is frequently the better pedagogical approach, while starting with philosophy and investigating the educational implications of the philosophical principle(s) is the more logical avenue. The examples to follow are ordered fundamentally according to the philosophical topics; in them the philosophical principles of Harris are explained and the consequences for his educational theory then are elaborated with some effort to clarify the relationship between the two.[12]

General Nature of the Human Person and Education

One of the most general statements in Harris's Annual Reports concerning the nature of the human person is based on a philosophical distinction of Aristotle: "first entelechy" designates the undeveloped human being; "second entelechy" signifies the developed, cultured person. The former is rational only potentially, while the latter is rational actually. The possibility of becoming rational (and more fully human) occurs through intellectual, moral, and religious formation based on self-activity. "The nature of man is realized in the angelic God-like being, whose intellect, and will, and emotions are rational, moral, and pervaded by love."[13] This view of the person presumes, of course, a dualistic being of matter and spirit. Such a position can be attributed to Harris on the basis of his remark (in the context of a discussion concerning education) that "in nature everything corresponds to spirit, and hence each lower material object is in some sense a key to unlock the perception of a higher, more subtle object."[14]

A broad educational purpose which is seen by Harris as a consequence of this general view of the person is "the harmonious development of human nature, physical, intellectual, moral and affectional."[15] A more specific, but pertinent, educational matter lies in the inclusion of reading and writing among elementary studies in order to free the student from "the circumscribed life of the senses," in which he is confined to a narrow circle of persons (and objects, he might add) as a step toward confronting "the world at large."[16]

Another aspect of Harris's philosophy of education in his Annual Reports is focused upon the transition stage of the child from ages four through six and its implications for kindergarten education. The child during these years is experiencing personal individuality as well as the desire for socialization. The latter is evident in an interest in children of a similar age outside the home and in the activities of people in "the great world of civil society," which are mimicked in his games. On the side of developing individuality, the child becomes aware of his own tendencies and learns to exercise his own will, as distinct from merely complying with the wishes of elders. At this stage, however, self-will tends to be capricious and arbitrary (and, to that extent, anti-social), as Harris sees it.[17]

What do the budding conscious inclinations of the child toward individuality and socialization mean for education? What bearing or impact do these developing human dimensions have upon the efforts of educators? The level of education involved here is the kindergarten, for which Harris is justly famous as an innovator.[18] Regarding the need of the child for socialization, it is clear that the mere fact of schooling provides a means to that end. Relative to individuality, the kindergarten, as well as education everywhere, is "to secure the maximum of self-activity in the pupil." To Harris this is the "first principle of pedagogy," namely, "that the pupil is educated, not by what others do for him, but by what he is led to do for himself."[19] Furthermore, the kindergarten is intended to "furnish an initiation into the arts and sciences" in a "manner half playful, half serious," which is such that it "balances" the promotion of the child's arbitrary will with the rational order of the school.[20] At this point the educational process is supposed to begin to moderate individuality in the direction of socialization. The kindergarten also is responsible for promoting the development of the physical aptitude of the child for manual skill.[21]

Another dimension of the person which is considered briefly and related in a general way to education is nationalistic background and interest. Harris claims that national memories and aspirations, family traditions and customs, and moral and religious observances form what may be called the substance of human character; as such, they cannot be removed or changed suddenly without "disastrously weakening the personality."[22] This provides part of the basis for the introduction of German language classes into the schools.[23]

The next two examples of Harris's philosophy of education in his Annual Reports to be explicated here pertain to broad perspectives on human development and implications for some aspect of education. Assuming that "In one sense the whole of life is an education," there are clearly defined epochs of growth: infancy, youth, and post-school age.[24] Corresponding agencies of education are the family, the school, and "apprenticeship to a vocation or calling in life." In the family, the child forms habits concerning personal care and conduct; and in the school, the youth cultivates certain intellectual and moral habits. Other educational agencies include the state, wherein the person functions as a citizen, and the church, which assists him to learn "to see all things under the form of eternity, and to derive thence the ultimate standards of his theory and practice in life."[25]

In another statement concerning human development, implications for the curriculum are noted. Table 1 depicts Harris's view in this regard.[26]

These epochs of development are said by Harris to be "well marked" in terms of "mental emancipation." Curriculum construction becomes a vital factor in human maturation since "An attempt to force the mind into a higher stage of activity before the body is prepared for it may produce a dwarfed development and delay a healthy growth for a long period."[27]

Table 1.

Birth to 7 years of age	Childhood	Symbolical stage	An initiation into the arts and sciences in kindergarten
7 to 13/14	Boyhood or and girlhood	Conventional stage	For example, reading writing
13/14 to . . .	Youth	Generalizing stage	Algebra, grammar, physical geography, physics, etc.[58]

A final example of Harris's philosophy of education in these Annual Reports relative to "the person, in general" is focused upon the final cause or the essence of human life, which is identified with "the participation by the individual in the life of the whole."[28] This participation is physical and applies to productive industry; more significantly, however, it is spiritual and pertains to imperishable ideas and aspirations. By means of the latter type of participation, the "puny individual" employs "his infinite nature, his reason" to become potentially all mankind and a being of infinite worth. "To reveal this rational nature that works in each one as an individual and still more visibly in society as a whole, or in the movements of the World History—is the final cause of our struggle."[29]

Since participation in the highest life (as that embodied in art, religion, and the sciences) is essential to every person, the means to this end also are essential. The means mentioned explicitly in this context are the invention of letters and of moveable types, the printing press, the telegraph, the daily newspaper, the book, the library, and the reading room—all educational instruments.[30] The library rates special notice here as "the temple dedicated to the communion of man, as an individual, with man, as a generic existence." Through it a person can become familiar with the wisdom of the ages by studying science, philosophy, religious writings and the Scriptures.[31] These subjects also indicate, of course, prominent elements of a curriculum.

In this section on the nature of the person, in general, and educational implications, six examples of Harris's philosophy of education were discussed on the basis of his Annual Reports. The person as a potentially and actually rational being was related to a broad educational purpose; the individual and social development of the child was related to a purpose and an aspect of the curriculum of the kindergarten; the substance of human character was related to the curriculum for ethnic education; two versions of human development were related to agencies of education and the curriculum, respectively; and the final cause or essence of life was related to several means of education and some subjects of the curriculum.

This "human person, in general" which has been considered has several key characteristics, including the following: a thinking, knowing being; an individual and social being; a free, self-active being; a moral being; and a religious being. Some attention will be given to Harris's views of each of these features, and to one or more educational implications of each as he describes them.

The Human Mind and Education

The framework for this aspect of Harris's philosophy of education is suggested in the following observation: "In each direction in which the human mind can grow healthfully there is progress to be made in some representative study."[32] With this remark, he is promoting philosophical investigation into the nature of the mind as a basis for formulating the curriculum. Because of the nature of the mind, not only should certain subjects (such as mathematics) be studied, but there is a definite order to be followed among subjects and within a subject area.[33] According to Harris, the first impressions of the intellectual milieu upon the young person "have sometimes the power to change and fix the whole bent of the mind."[34] Therefore, it is desirable that, at the outset of formal education, the student should be confronted with subject matter which is logically consistent, methodical, and philosophical.[35]

While these interpretations exemplify Harris's philosophy of education in this area in a very general manner, they do not depict its specific drift. Clarifying the latter requires a review of his version of thinking. There are three stages in the process of human cognition, and they are associated with the three faculties of perception, understanding, and reason. In the first stage the sensible object or property is isolated through the attention of the agent; secondly, it is abstracted and reunited with its necessary relations through processes of reflection and analysis; and, finally, its universality and necessity are perceived by a comprehension (intuition) or synthesis of its wholeness. While analysis dominates in the realm of understanding and synthesis at the stage of reason, neither is found to the exclusion of the other. The end result of these three levels of self-activity, the higher of which envelops the lower in each case, is an appreciation of universal and necessary truths, called "intuitive truths" or "intuitive ideas" (as, for example, God, freedom, and immortality).[36] This cognitive process is summarized in Table 2.

In a sense, application of this philosophical dissection of the process of human thought to education is brief and preliminary in the immediate context.

Table 2.

Faculty	Processor Function	Object
Perception	Attention	Isolated properties
Understanding	Analysis/Reflection	Abstractions and relations (Relativity)
Reason	Classifications Comprehension (Intuition) Synthesis	Totalities or wholes

On the other hand, the whole description is educationally-oriented; it is initiated with the assertion that "Intellectual training in the school begins with the habit of attention."[37] In other words, while the teaching-learning process in a school environment is mentioned directly only at the beginning, the entire passage is portrayed as a school endeavor. However, this lengthy description of thinking can be considered as a philosophical explanation needing to be elaborated in relationship to its educational consequences in order to be viewed more fully as an example of philosophy of education. This academic discipline is exemplified in the text, according to this interpretation, by relating this "meaning of mind" to what is said about initiating intellectual formation in the school by inculcating the habit of attention. For, without exercising the will (the human spiritual faculty by means of which one makes choices) to "attend to" a selected physical object or group of objects, the intellect (the human spiritual faculty of knowing) will not be engaged in the higher cognitive processes of understanding and reasoning.[38]

Further educational implications of this process of intellection can be observed in the following examples of Harris's philosophy of education. In a somewhat lengthy critique of Pestalozzi's "object-lesson" system, Harris elaborates some educational features of his own view of human cognition. This example can be initiated with the following citation: "Give man the tools of thought and he will immediately invent the tools of art, and forthwith conquer nature. What we attempt in school education is precisely that very thing—the giving to the pupil skill to handle the tools of thought."[39] These two sentences represent the seeds of a fully blossomed epistemology of education; the first one refers (in part) to the philosophy of mind, and the second is a statement of educational purpose, suggesting more specific purposes, a curriculum, teaching methods, etc.

The question of teaching methods is broached by Harris immediately following the two sentences just cited. He seriously objects to methods which are intended to rivet the attention of the student exclusively upon physical objects as if that process represented the true and only means of learning. His objection is founded upon his philosophical conviction that universal, necessary truths, which are real and apprehensible, cannot be known in this way. Truths such as those concerning God, freedom, and immortality "require the profound reflection of the soul into itself. The mind must arise out of the senses and the external—the inward light must shine so that by its mild radiance the Eternal Verities may become visible."[40] Therefore, "the object-lesson system [of Pestalozzi] . . . completely inverts the relation of the knower to the known; instead of giving the mind the tools to subdue and dissolve the external fact with, it tells us rather that the external fact is the true already, by which we must mould the mind."[41] Harris also attacks, on similar grounds, educators who advocate teaching methods focused exclusively on discipline or exercise of the mind as if it were a muscle. The representatives of this educational heresy contend that the *manner* of thought is all-important, and that one can be indifferent to *what* the student studies. The result is the cultivation of attention as a goal and "amassing lumber yards and stone quarries of atomic facts."[42]

Harris's own theory of knowledge leads him to assert that "To free oneself from the thralldom of the senses and arrive at clear reflection and comprehensive reasoning is the desideratum; hence the teaching which starts with sensuous objects will do best when it elevates its pupils soonest above the need of such aids to secure attention."[43] The content of education is formed in terms of the "conventionalities of intelligence." *What* one studies is as important as *how* it is studied. Furthermore, this content should be chosen in light of the fact that "that knowledge of most value" has the widest application. For this reason, education must be limited to "the acquirement of principles," leaving their application to the practice gained in one's vocation. This position suggests the following principle of curriculum construction: "We should give general culture so far as we give any, and postpone as long as possible the selection of the special avocation, so that the selection may be made after there has been the fullest opportunity to develop the peculiar fitness of the individual, and the individual himself has become mature as possible—able to select his own avocation."[44] Harris then lists the following studies as the basis of education:

"I. Reading, Writing, Arithmetic, Geography, Grammar, and History.
II. Algebra and Geometry, the study of Latin, German or French, Natural Philosophy (Physics),—these come next.
III. Afterwards special sciences—such as Chemistry, Physiology, Geology, Botany, Astronomy—the higher Mathematics, Greek, Literature, Mental and Moral Philosophy, Aesthetics."[45]

This example of Harris's philosophy of mind in relationship to educational purposes, the curriculum and (negatively, at least) teaching methods obviously relies heavily upon the details of the process of human cognition explained in the previous example.

The following brief examples can be viewed as extensions of the last two. The mastery of any province of knowledge involves the three stages (the perceptive, the reflective, and the stage of insight) undertaken at a pace suited for "complete assimilation." These three graduated levels of awareness, entailing the faculties of perception, understanding, and reason, respectively, cannot occur simultaneously since each, in turn, relies upon the previous one.[46] Therefore, the course of study should be sufficiently exhaustive at each of its "epochs" to allow for this assimilation of principles. What the mind "acquires in its early stages will be rudimentary, but will furnish a rich native store for future thought when the period of reflection sets in stronger and stronger." Therefore, Harris's curriculum tends to be repetitious, but in a manner conducive to promoting a deepened awareness of reality commensurate with the three stages of knowing. Education, then, is responsible for "a period of estrangement from the common and familiar," meaning that "The pupil must be led out of his immediateness and separated in spirit from his naturalness, in order that he may be able to return from his self-estrangement to the world that lies nearest to him, and consciously seize and master it." Not totally unlike the occurrence in Plato's analogy of the cave,[47] the student transcends his awareness of material objects to comprehend "higher realities," returning to view the physical in a renewed manner. For Harris this self-estrangement entails not only removal from the concrete to the abstract and universal, but also from the modern world to the "distant world of classical antiquity."[48] Therefore, we have another example of how Harris's theory of mind and theory of knowledge affect the direction of the process of education and the curriculum.

In still another example of his philosophy of education pertaining to epistemology, Harris distinguishes two levels of education. On the philosophical side, he asserts that "Every conscious intellectual phase of the mind has a previous phase in which it was unconscious, and merely symbolic."[49] The symbolic phase, activities of the soul called feeling, emotion or sensibility, becomes the former, namely, thoughts and ideas. The feelings, impulses or instincts are pre-existing ideas, in a sense. They are particular, or applicable in specific circumstances, whereas the ideas are "general principles regulative of all similar exigencies."[50]

This philosophical distinction provides the foundation for the use of the nursery tale in early formal education; the story provides the elements of a thought, but in such manner that the child grasps only the incident. Subsequent reflection crystallizes the features previously detached and isolated, and the child begins to formulate a general idea. "The previous symbol makes easy and natural the pathway to ideas and clear thought."[51] Furthermore, future intellectual growth is enhanced through attention in early education to the cultivation of imagination and "the inventive power" along with habits of regularity, punctuality, silence, obedience to established rules, and self-control.[52] Furthermore, noting the development of an interest in "the problem of life" in youth of high school and college ages, Harris points to the corresponding rise of the power of insight (or reason), whereby the universality and necessity of principles can be known. This gives the mission of the high school: to develop in the student insight and directive power enabling graduates to assume leadership in the community.[53]

A final example of philosophy of education concerning the human mind and education pertains directly to all of the other examples in this section. Harris says that "The culture of the rational soul — the intellect, the will, and the affections — is the privilege of every human being, *whether male or female*. More than this it is a duty . . ." (emphasis mine).[54] Ideas and directive power are neither male nor female, but characteristic of *all* human beings.[55] Therefore, a similar "higher end" for male and female, and vocational preparation similar for each are given as reasons supporting the same course of study for both sexes.[56]

In summary of this section concerning the human mind and education, according to Harris in his Annual Reports, the philosophical keynote is the three-stage process of cognition by means of which the person gains an awareness of physical objects (through perception) as a basis for developing both an appreciation of abstractions and relationships (through the understanding), and a comprehension of universal truths (through reason). For education this signifies the necessity of 1) promoting the student's self-activity through all three stages (an *educational purpose*); 2) teaching him general principles (rather than practical applications) based in several specific subjects (the *curriculum*); and 3) avoiding exclusive attention to a) discipline of the mind (attended by an indifference to subject matter) and b) object-lessons (*teaching methods*). Other implications for education pertain to the responsibility of the educator for inducing the "self-estrangement" of the student, and to a distinction between early formal education and the high school. A final example of philosophy of education in this section depicts the male-female relationship as a basis for suggesting the need for co-education and for requiring the same course of study for both sexes.

A bond between the examples of philosophy of education in this section and those in the first section (concerning the nature of the person, in general, and education) is seen in the dualisms underlying both. The human person is a being of matter and spirit, body and soul; and the soul has faculties of will (for choosing) and intellect (for knowing). Furthermore, the human person is an individual and a social being, a distinction under direct scrutiny in the next section.

Human Socialization and Education

The topic of human socialization, concerning matters of social and political philosophy, is intimately associated with epistemology, according to Harris. Therefore, one could expect an affinity between the educational theories deriving from each of these two areas of his philosophy.

Human socialization is manifested both physically and spiritually. Harris states categorically that "The wants of a man as a physical being are all mediated through his relation to society."[57] Food, shelter, and clothing are mentioned explicitly as derived from the energies of society, in which the individual is to lose himself in order to rediscover himself. The contributions of the individual toward the welfare of society are returned to him by the social aggregate through its organization.[58] However, socialization extends beyond the realm of the physical. "This interchange, brought about through the division of labor, and commerce, is the corner-stone of civilization—an exchange not merely of the elements of food and clothing, but of arts, institutions, and ideas."[59]

Because the individual person depends upon society directly, finding it to be the presupposition of his existence, "it happens that education busies itself chiefly with initiating the individual into the conventionalities of society."[60] This formation should begin at birth with an acquisition of the "general habits" of fellow persons. The school, however, has a special role in this process, the role of bringing to consciousness the elements underlying this social organism. The school has the unique function of giving "to each individual the language of that social organization, and the common stock of ideas which govern it," "the theoretical tools by which he obtains the mastery over the realms of nature as well as over those of mind."[61]

The order of education is the mastery of language (that is, the usages of the social whole), which is a means to mastery of the material world. Regarding the order of the curriculum, Harris sees this as a partial reason for exposing the student to the human sciences prior to the natural sciences. Although it is more important for the person to know human nature than material nature, he should be ignorant of neither.[62] The five elementary branches of reading and writing, arithmetic, geography, history, and grammar are each expanded in the high school, following the "same symmetry of system."[63] These studies are of "infinitely more importance" than any others because "the pupil who is taught how to master these subjects is at the same time taught how to master all branches of human learning."[64] Therefore, in this example of Harris's philosophy of education, certain principles of his social philosophy are applied to the purposes of education with special attention to the goals of the school, as such, and to the curriculum.

The second example of Harris's social philosophy in its relationship to education in his Annual Reports is initiated (on the philosophical side) by pointing out the need to "balance" the human tendencies toward spontaneity and prescription. The person is a spontaneous being, needing to follow his own instincts, who also must learn obedience and self-sacrifice in order to prepare for "a life of combination with his fellow-men."[65] Through social institutions, the basis of which is language, the results of all individuals are able to be shared mutually. This pertains to the physical products of human labor and to human experience.[66]

One obvious educational implication of this philosophical position is the necessity to inculcate obedience in the student. Self-discipline must be fostered through the acquisition of habits of regularity, punctuality, silence, neatness, courtesy, kindness, liberality, truthfulness, patience, self-denial, and industry. This moral education must be complemented by intellectual education, of course, in which the student is to acquire the faculties of attention, perception, memory, reflection, and insight. In light of the nature of the person, the educator must exercise extraordinary caution to avoid, on one hand, promoting excessive self-indulgence in the student with inordinate permissiveness, and, on the other hand, crushing individuality with an overemphasis on obedience. Harris concludes that "If the individual can retain his originality and freshness and yet acquire the habits that are necessary for combination with his fellow-men, he becomes a truly educated human being."[67]

Harris's philosophy of education in the area of socialization also is exemplified (thirdly) by his comments on human genius and originality in relationship to educational purposiveness and teaching methodology. His familiar theme is that "the greater part of life is after all the participation in the life of the race and its assimilation, rather than exclusively original experience."[68] Concerning both the physical and the spiritual realms of human living, "The race transcends the individual almost in an infinite potency." For this reason, genius is "the ascent of the individual into the vision and will-power of the race—so that he is guided by the universality of mankind, and is a fit guide for others."[69] Negative features of failing to participate in the common experiences of the race include gaining an unrealistic view of the world, mistaking idiosyncrasy for originality, and exhibiting erratic and fruitless behavior. To support his contention, Harris points to the fact that the original contributions of each of the greatest scientists are noticeably meager relative to what each one learned from others.[70]

The educational implications of these philosophical considerations are very important to Harris. In fact, "the school has its chief work in initiating the pupil into the accumulated wisdom of the race as a preliminary to his original additions to the same."[71] This statement of educational direction suggests to Harris two basic methods of teaching: textbook lessons and independent experiment or original investigation.[72] The latter method is the "new avatar in education" and, according to Harris, has been overemphasized by some to the detriment of educational achievement. He sees the need for utilizing both methods in a suitable balance. Although in early life the assimilating stage (and, therefore, the textbook method) predominates; and during the more mature years, the stage of original acquisition (and the method of independent experiment) comes to the fore, neither method can replace the other. The textbook method should not be underestimated as a means of introducing the student to the experience of mankind; however, the method of investigation "does not, when rightly understood, conflict with the method of critical comparison of authorities, but is a valuable supplement to it. . . ."[73] This educational position seems to reflect clearly Harris's conception of the development of true originality and genius in light of his general theory of human socialization.

The next two examples of Harris's philosophy of education in the area of human socialization are directed more immediately to social institutions, as such, with implications for the school curriculum and (in one case) the public school library. According to Harris, "human nature is revealed in and by means of institutions alone." These institutions are "combinations or organizations of man, united under the direction of an ideal." Language, an institution itself, is the "primary condition . . . out of which institutions develop." It is "the visible image or realization of reason," an essential means to a revelation of human nature and to scientific knowledge which signify a transcendence of nature. By means of "fixing" the transient and variable, language provides the basis for the universalization of meaning and the sharing of experiences among human beings.[74]

This view of the role of institutions (including language) in human development obviously affects the curriculum. In fact, the study of language "as a mere thing is more important and profitable than the study of any other thing in time and space."[75] Alongside language, which is a necessary means to the spiritual combination of persons, is mathematics, which is directly useful in "natural combination," or the production of material goods by the social organism. These two studies, being fundamental to human socialization and to culture, as such, "form the two essential branches of intellectual education in the school."[76] Teaching methodology also is touched upon here as an educational consequence of the above view of social institutions since "The printed page contains the oracles of the race."[77] Therefore, the basic subjects (reading, arithmetic, geography, grammar and history) are intended to assist the student to master a subject by studying it in a book. This also suggests the role of the public school library, "the museum for the preservation of the results of human labor and experience as embodied in language."[78]

The last example of Harris's philosophy of education highlighting social institutions on the philosophical side is focused upon the family, civil society, and the state. (The church, the corporation, and the army also are mentioned.) These institutions "are only different forms of existence of man's self; they are his greater selves, which unfold one by one from him as he lives through time, and combines with his fellow-men to form these social organisms or institutions."[79] The ability to see man's greater selves, as identified with these institutions, is the faculty of the human mind called insight.

The cultivation of insight to allow for the kind of vision described is the responsibility of the process of education. The school curriculum is an immediate concern.[80] In this curriculum which is developed in light of the nature and function of these designated social institutions, history is extremely important because it introduces the student into "the method of thinking about the deeds of man in their relations to his institutions, not as causes simply, nor as effects simply, but as in reciprocal action—as producers and produced."[81] Other basic subjects mentioned above are also recommended. Mathematics and the natural sciences provide directive power over matter and the possibility of combining things and forces (presumably for the production of material goods). Language, literature and history endow the student with insight into human nature, enabling him to appreciate the combination of persons and the rise of social institutions.[82] Natural science is for the more mature student, and it, as well as history, should be taught not through textbooks, but by means of "recitation." In these classes, the teacher is to proceed dialectically, ascertaining the awareness of the students, arousing reflection, and promoting the development of the ability to see relationships.[83] This teaching method and the curriculum suggested are intended to effect in the students the knowledge and activity necessary to the building of the human race through social institutions.

The sixth example of Harris's philosophy of education based upon the philosophical topic of human socialization centers upon the consideration of a pluralistic democracy. In regard to democracy, Harris insists upon providing each child, regardless of social class, an opportunity to become intelligent and virtuous. He prescribes the eradication of "caste distinctions" and the development of homogeneity based upon "educated intelligence."[84] The pluralistic dimension of democracy pertains to the national (German, in this case) memories and aspirations, customs and habits, and moral and religious observances which form the substance of the character of each person. Sudden removal or alteration of these structures results in disastrous effects upon the personality.[85]

These principles of Harris's socio-political philosophy bear immediate consequences for education. First of all, "The public school is the instrumentality designed for the conservation of true democratic principles."[86] To this end, it is to eliminate class distinctions, "perhaps, the most important function of the public school."[87] Secondly, the curriculum is affected by the introduction of the foreign language(s) involved; in this instance, German is to be introduced to promote a thorough mingling of nationalities and the abolition of social classes.[88] Therefore, in this example it is clear that Harris's conception of pluralistic democracy yields prescriptions for the direction and the curriculum of a school.

The seventh example of Harris's philosophy of education in the Annual Reports which belongs to this heading of socialization tends to be an epitome of the others. Harris capsulizes the central philosophical theme of this section when he says that "The essential in human life consists in the participation by the individual in the life of the whole."[89] This participation, as has been noted, is material and spiritual. A key difference between these two kinds of participation lies in the perishable feature of the products of the former and the imperishable character of the entities involved in the latter. Ideas become more potent as they are shared: "The one who communicates an idea to his fellow man knows it better for having communicated it, and the one who learns it, instead of depriving anyone else of his share of it, thereby assists others to share it."[90] Harris likens this spiritual process to the miracle of Christ in feeding the multitude in Galilee. He concludes this passage with an ode to human reason: "It is his [the human person's] infinite nature, his reason, that which makes him—a puny individual—potentially all mankind; that which makes the soul of the weakest a somewhat of infinite worth. To reveal this rational nature that works in each one as an individual and still more visibly in society as a whole, or in the movements of the World History—is the final cause of our struggles."[91]

Since participation in the highest life (as embodied in art, religion, and science) is necessary to the realization of the person and to his distinction from the brute animal, the means to this end also are necessary, and "their establishment is to be regarded as the highest deed in the practical world."[92] These means, according to Harris, include such educational tools as the printing press, the telegraph, the daily newspaper, the book, and the library. The library is noted especially in this context; it is referred to as "the temple dedicated to the communion of man, as an individual, with man, as a generic existence."[93] This statement brings the printed page and education for the use of it into focus as a key to human socialization, which is necessary to living a rational life.

The final example of Harris's philosophy of education in the Annual Reports under the heading of human socialization pertains to all of the others in this section. It is asserted that the ascent of the individual into the conscious participation with the race as a whole requires a struggle on the part of each person. (This observation is made in the context of a discussion of the importance of aspiration in human development and the roles of unhappiness as well as happiness in that development.)[94] Consequent educational goals are "to arm and equip the individual to realize this and to give him as much aspiration as possible for an impelling power."[95]

A central theme of this section on Harris's social and political philosophy and its implications for education is the necessity of the individual to participate physically and spiritually with others through social organizations in order to become truly human. The spiritual side of this combination is the more important, and, therefore, holds a greater significance for the establishment of the purposes of education, the curriculum, and teaching methods, including the use of various educational instruments such as the daily newspaper and the library. Table 3 sketches the main emphases in the eight examples of Harris's philosophy of education in this section.

Table 3.

1) The process of socialization—as physical and spiritual	1) Purposes of education, purposes of schooling, the curriculum
2) Socialization as a process of "balancing" spontaneity and prescription	2) Purposes of moral and intellectual education
3) Socialization as a means to genuine originality and genius	3) Purposes of the school, methods of teaching
4) The necessity of social institutions for socialization, and the role of language for sharing universalized meaning	4) The curriculum, public school library
5) Specific social institutions in the process of socialization	5) The curriculum, methods of teaching
6) Pluralistic democracy and socialization	6) Purposes of education, curriculum
7) (Summary) The essence of the person as found in participation with others, a physical and spiritual process	7) Essential means to include such educational instruments as the printed page and, especially, the library.
8) (Conclusion) The personal struggle and effort required for human combination	8) Purposes of education

Human Freedom and Education

One purpose of human socialization is human freedom; therefore, education for socialization also must exist to promote freedom. As a result, the following examples of philosophy of education according to William Torrey Harris in his Annual Reports are closely allied with those in the previous section (which, as has been seen, are intimately associated with those in the first two sections). All four of the major examples in this section pertain to the individual-social aspect of the person in some manner, but only the first focuses directly upon the national and governmental dimension of life.

In this first example, the "national idea of self-government and independence for each individual" is taken as a starting point or basis in discussing education.[96] The course of study in the school, Harris says, follows this position by aiming to provide each student, as early as possible, with the means of acquiring information on his own. The educational principle involved is the following: "'Not what the teacher does for the pupil directly, but what he gets the pupil to do for himself, is of value.'"[97] The instrument suggested to attain this end is the textbook, which enables the teacher to discuss the "General relations of the subject" while presuming the student's familiarity with certain details gained from the book.[98] Therefore, the preparation of independent persons who also are competent to govern themselves as a nation is the responsibility of the school, which employs teachers who instill habits of thinking with the help of textbooks.

The second example of "human freedom and education" addresses the nature of freedom in a rather broad fashion, with general implications for educational ends and means. The background for the nature of human freedom lies in the conception of human nature, according to Harris. "Nature" has various meanings: 1) the external world (of unconscious growth and dependence); 2) the lower, animalistic, instinctive (and, thus, unconscious and dependent) dimension of man, and 3) the higher or rational (and free) side of man. The last is identified with "human nature" in the fullest sense, and underlies Harris's assertion that "the nature of man—human nature—must be freedom, and not fate."[99] The human being, as such, is not a thing, determined by "the constraining activity of the totality of conditions; rather, the person is self-determined, will-power being the source of his freedom."[100] Human freedom or self-determination is achieved through becoming rational, which is accomplished (at least partially) by the substitution of moral purpose for mere impulse or instinct, a process also known as the practice of self-control. The desired result of (and means to) these means is "participation with others" or socialization. In this context, Harris says, "Through participation with his fellow-men united into institutions—those infinite, rational organisms, the product of the intellect and will of the race conspiring through the ages of human history and inspired by the Divine purpose which rules all Providence—through participation in institutions, man is enabled to attain freedom, to complement his defects as individual by the deeds of the race...."[101] In a related passage located in proximity to the above, the wisest men are said to be those who "have availed themselves most of the wisdom of the race." The assimilation of the intellectual patrimony is due essentially not only to self-activity, but also to a "reverent spirit" (necessary for sustaining one in the enduring effort to acquire that heritage).[102] The implicit contrast between self-activity and a reverent spirit apparently coincides to some extent with what has been referred to as impulse and self-control, respectively.[103]

What is suggested for the process of education by the fact that a human being becomes free through becoming rational in participation with others? The general direction of education is of immediate concern. Practically considered, education is "a process of initiating the particular individual into the life of his race as intellect and will-power. We must give to a child the means to help himself, and the habit and custom of helping himself, to participate in the labors of his fellowmen, and to become a contributor to the store created by mankind."[104] The general object of the kindergarten, or entry level in formal education, is "to eliminate the merely animal from the child, and to develop in its place the rational and spiritual life" (an end identified with that of all school education).[105] The agencies of education responsible for implementing this goal are the family, the civil society (including schools), the state, and the church.[106] Since will-power is the source of freedom, which is actualized when irrational arbitrariness and caprice are transformed into rational planning and activity, the school must strive to "balance" the cultivation of spontaneity and obedience in the most beneficial manner possible. Spontaneity is identified with play and obedience with work. The kindergarten prescribes or controls "wisely and gently" so as "to leave room for much of the pure spontaneity of play. It prescribes tasks, but preserves the form of play as much as in possible."[107] This "balance" and the mode of inspiring it would vary at various levels of schooling, always with the aim of preventing capriciousness as well as mindless subjugation. In this example, it is evident that Harris's view of freedom, based upon his conception of human nature, especially the role of reason and participation with others in social institutions, is directly related to his perspective on the general direction of education and certain means to be taken within it, as well as to educational agencies.

The third example of Harris's philosophy of education in his Annual Reports relative to freedom and education is directed specifically to the correlative aspects of freedom and implications for pedagogical purposes and methodology. One dimension of freedom is *absolute toleration*, "which permits and encourages differences of opinion, and trusts that the freest exercise of thought is the healthiest, and will lead in the surest way to the absolute truth wherein all convictions shall be united in one."[108] The other dimension is *subordination to law*, "wherein each man squares his deeds by the universal rules laid down in the statute books, and prescribed by the judicial function of the government—wherein each man not only squares his own deeds by the universal norm, but at the same time insists that each and every other man shall square his deed by the same norm."[109] These two provinces (also called spontaneity and prescription, respectively) interpenetrate to delimit general human progress, which is measured by "free thought taking up and comprehending the prescriptions embodied in the institutions of civilizations."[110] In other words, the ideal calls for mandates which shed their external, mechanical, and tyrannical side as their necessary foundation is comprehended. The external character of social institutions melts away as their essential character becomes known and affirmed or accepted with complete conviction. The free person has attained this comprehension and (presumably) has exercised this affirmation. "At the highest point spontaneity and prescription have reached the same content or subject matter, and the individual finds prescription and conviction requiring the same thing."[111]

How does this version of freedom affect education? Insofar as the school is the "theatre" for the transition of obedience to external authority into free action on the basis of personal conviction, it must resolve the paradox of spontaneity and prescription (referred to as "the perpetual problem before us").[112] The aim is the development of a person "free and progressive without omitting to recognize and preserve the immense depth and breadth of the institutions developed from his history and embodying the substance of his being, unfolded in time."[113] This end seems to conjure up the notions of attention to the past and investigations into the present. In this regard, Harris recommends the use of a textbook, not to promote unquestioned "parrot-like repetition of the words of the book," but to develop in the student "the most rapid mental independence."[114] This kind of freedom is learned through the student's efforts to compare differing statements and views in a book (or several books), and to verify his ideas by consulting various authorities and by exhausting sources of information on a particular subject. An important principle underlying this method refers to the question of the past and present: "Original investigation should not so much precede as follow a mastery of what has already been accomplished." For example, the student should become familiar with past discoveries in electricity or chemistry before undertaking to advance its status through investigation.[115] The teaching method called "class-recitation" is mentioned as a means of reviewing and previewing subject matter, and of assisting the student to relate details, to remember important points, and to develop habits of thought.[116] Details and a general overview of the subject matter should be clear to the student.[117]

A brief version of this basic example, relating the two correlative aspects of freedom to certain purposes and methods of teaching, also is seen in another Annual Report of Harris. Here (in summary of the above example) it is stated that the "yokelessness of caprice and arbitrariness is the illusive semblance of freedom."[118] Lack of restraint or freedom from subordination to reason must give way to compliance with rules and laws which are essential to human combination, which, in turn, is so vital to personal development.[119] Education must take account of this matter at all levels. However, "the pressure of prescription must be adjusted so delicately that it will not crush out his individuality in his tender age . . . nor lack sufficient force to secure conformity in his later youth."[120] The proper balance must be sought persistently.

The final example of Harris's philosophy of freedom in relationship to education revolves around freedom through self-knowledge and implications for the school curriculum. The first requirement for "directive power" is knowledge. "Directive intelligence, knowledge itself, may ceaselessly modify the effects of its presuppositions as it finds them on itself, and by successive acts of the will may determine itself in accordance with its pure ideal. This is freedom."[121] Therefore, to consciously possess oneself or to govern one's own life, a person must gain self-knowledge. This kind of knowledge, as any scientific knowledge, requires awareness of the pertinent historical background. Applied to the human person, this means that "The man who does not know his history nor the history of his civilization, does not consciously possess himself."[122] Knowing oneself through history, as intended here, is achieved only by means of "living through" that history, which cannot be accomplished in reading translations of the culture's history or literature. "The thorough assimilation of it [one's history] in consciousness demands such an immediate contact with it as one gets by learning the languages of these people—the clothing of their inmost spiritual selves."[123] In this regard, Harris notes that Western Civilization stemmed from Greece and Rome[124] which stand at the entrance to the modern world or the Occidental phase in world history."[125] Greece introduced into history the idea of individuality, and Rome deepened that notion to one of the legal person. From Greek science, Roman laws, and Christianity were derived national independence and a human civilization.[126]

The educational conclusion bearing on the curriculum is obvious: Greek and Latin should be included in the curriculum[127] in order to provide for the genuine possibility of self-knowledge, which is requisite to authentic liberty. Greek provides the presuppositions of the theoretical intelligence and Latin the presuppositions of the practical side of intelligence. Learning Greek and Latin allow one to "live through" one's own cultural past enroute to enhanced self-knowledge and freedom. Attendant values of these classical studies are discipline, culture, exactness of thought, and refining influence; they contribute to "the conscious possession of the conventionalities of our civilization."[128] In this final example of Harris concerning freedom and education, the classical language components of the curriculum have been seen to be founded on his view of freedom through self-knowledge, which can be gained only by means of "living through" one's cultural history, that of Greece and Rome in this case.

Four major examples were brought forth in this section in an attempt to clarify the philosophy of education of Harris in his Annual Reports relative to his understanding of human freedom and its consequences for education. The educational implications centered primarily upon the purposes of education, the curriculum, and teaching methods, with one reference to educational agencies. These pedagogical conclusions were drawn from 1) an assertion of the reality of the independence of the individual person and national self-government; 2) a view of human freedom based upon a notion of the person emphasizing the rational and social dimensions; 3) an explanation of two correlative aspects of freedom, spontaneity and prescription; and 4) comments on freedom through self-knowledge.

Morality (and Religion) and Education

Although morality and moral education have not been omitted entirely from all of the foregoing examples of philosophy of education of William Torrey Harris in his Annual Reports, they deserve special treatment in relationship to one another in this context. Three examples will be analyzed, the first being merely introductory. The second example focuses exclusively upon morality and moral education, while the third one brings the second into relationship with religion and the impact upon the school. Within this third example, advertence to Harris's philosophy of religion and religious education foreshadows the final section of the paper, religion and education.

In a very brief passage in one of his Annual Reports, Harris alludes to morality and two implications for the educator. He contrasts the four cardinal virtues (prudence, fortitude, temperance, and justice) with the seven deadly sins (which go unnamed): the former are based upon self-control in some form, while the latter represent various species of excess brought about by yielding to the appetites and passions.[129] This signifies that the student forms a moral basis for himself insofar as he "learns the lesson of self-denial and has acquired that energy of character which enables him to sacrifice the ease and pleasure of the moment in order to gain reasonable ends." Harris suggests that, perhaps, the most effective instrument in attaining this goal in the school is the strict enforcement of rules of attendance.[130] The relationship portrayed here between virtues and vices, on one hand, and the intent to inculcate in the students efforts toward self-sacrifice, on the other hand, foreshadows the central features of the second example, which elaborates the matter.

According to Harris, an "ethical system" is the "network of habits and observances which makes social combination possible, which enables men to live together as a community." The fundamental presupposition of all ethical systems is human responsibility,[131] and the feeling of responsibility constitutes the essence of virtue.[132] In line with this foundation, there are two classes of an individual's moral duties: duties to the self and duties to others. The former are responsibilities to actualize in one's self the ideal of humanity; the latter are responsibilities assumed primarily for the family, civil society, and the state.[133] In explaining this position, Harris claims that the fundamental basis of sound ethical principles is self-sacrifice, "employing as its conviction *responsibility*, i.e. the insight into the necessity of its own agency in attaining its true self by the suppression of its natural appetites." There are two sides or conditions of self-sacrifice, namely, obedience and kindness or love. Obedience is the general mode of conformity of the individual to general rules, laws, and prescribed forms of activity.[134] It has seven phases:

> 1) *punctuality* or conformity to the external requirements of time and place; 2) *order* and *regularity*—conformity to the rhythm that governs external things; 3) *perseverance*—conformity to purpose; 4) *earnestness*—conformity of outward endeavor to inward resolution; 5) *justice*—conformity to the universal (self-measured) standard of action; 6) *truthfulness*—conformity of utterance (speech and behavior) to reality; 7) *industry*—conformity of activity to the channels prescribed by society so that what one does is directly for others, indirectly for one's self.[135]

Kindness or love, the other side or condition of self-sacrifice, consists of various species: sympathy, forbearance, considerateness, mercy, benevolence, charity, and philanthropy. It views the person as embodying the ideal of humanity, the real final aim and destiny of the individual; and it attempts to remove the imperfections and limitations of humanity without injuring the individual.[136]

This perspective on morality bears extraordinary significance for the nature and importance of moral education According to Harris, "Morality is certainly indispensable to the system of education . . . morality must be provided for."[137] In fact, moral education is more important in the school than intellectual education: "Is there anything so evident as the fact that while the knowledge gained in school is of great importance, the discipline enforced there by proper means is far more important?"[138] The essence of this form of education is the training of the will.[139] It consists of the "initiation of the child into manners and customs, into the general forms of right doing—the conventionalities of civilization—... and it is the first necessity of the child when he grows up to the capacity of self-activity."[140] The sources or agencies of moral education are the family and the school. The family is responsible for the earliest formation of the child in the conduct of life, and is less scientific and more directly prescriptive than other subsequent moral influence. The nurture of the family provides the child with the first feeling of responsibility for self and the germ of true character.[141] As early as ages five or six, the child requires the mediation of "a more general training" and is sent to school.[142]

The discipline of the student through moral education is directed to the formation of habits such as punctuality, regularity, silence, truthfulness, justice, and kindness or love of mankind.[143] Punctuality is conformity to the requirements of time in particular instances: getting to school and observing guidelines and requirements while in school. Regularity is this conformity "made general." Punctuality and regularity are the most elementary obligations of the moral code, "its alphabet."[144] The school makes these indispensable (although not ultimate) duties the ground of and means to higher, spiritual culture.[145] The habit of silence is "the basis for the culture of internality or reflection." Its purposes are several: 1) to restrain the animal impulse to chatter, 2) to draw attention to the material environment, 3) to promote combination with others, 4) to improve the use of the memory, and 5) to allow for the awakening of insight and reflection. Harris calls silence "the soil in which thought grows."[146]

Truthfulness, another duty to be inculcated in the student, "is the basis of the duties of a human person toward others. No positive relation with our fellow men is .possible except through truth. Untruth is the essence of discord."[147] For this reason truth is fundamental to human development. Virtues resting on truth are earnestness and sincerity, and honesty and reliability; and vices founded on its neglect include lying, deceit, hypocrisy, cheating, and all "manners" of fraud. There are two means suggested for the school in its efforts to combat these vices which produce suspicion and distrust, and which stifle spiritual relationship: 1) requiring the student to be accurate and comprehensive in recitations, and 2) disciplining the student for transgression of the norms of truth.[148] The habit of justice is inculcated in the student by establishing a system of measure, conformity to rule and right being rewarded by recognition and breaches of discipline being met by prompt exposure. The student's attention, Harris says, should be turned to the distinction between "I want" and "I ought."[149] Lastly, kindness or love of mankind is the "highest virtue in our list." Requiring a community (as justice), its basis is the "feeling of justice fostered by a constant opportunity to see through the adventitious wrappings of social rank and condition and observe the real substance of the character."[150] These conditions suggest a broad human sympathy, which must be promoted in the school.[151] Other specific habits to be inculcated in the student through the process of moral education include industry, neatness, self-respect, obedience to rules, courtesy "and the like."[152]

In summary of Harris's theory of moral education, it is evident that discipline is the key. "It is clear that a school in which morality formed the staple of instruction . . . would be a fountain of moral corruption in the community, *unless strict discipline were maintained there*. It is the habitual practice of obedience to principle that constitutes morality."[153] Furthermore, "The discipline in our Public Schools, wherein . . . the pupils are continually taught to *suppress mere self-will* and inclination, is the best school of morality. Self-control is the basis of all moral virtues, and industrious and studious habits are the highest qualities we can form in our children."[154] In this central example relating principles of morality to moral education, according to Harris in this Annual Report, it has become clear that self-sacrifice, or responsibility for others, is the most fundamental principle of morality. This principle is to be understood and lived by the student by means of discipline, which is to be promoted at the initiative of the educator.

The third and last example of Harris's philosophy of education under this general heading brings morality into relationship with religion, and suggests further implications for moral education in the school. "Religion" here is that which defines the relation between the human person and God, and the conception of the final destiny of the person; it "contains the ultimate and supreme ground of all obligation."[155] On the philosophical side, there are two paradoxical points: the close relationship between morality and religion, and the separation of morality and religion. In regard to the first aspect of the paradox, it is clear that both morality and religion pertain directly to the notion of human obligation. Harris states the basic principle of *association* as follows: ". . . religion, containing as it does, the ultimate ground of obligation must necessarily furnish the ground for the system of ethics that grows up under it."[156] This obviously indicates a certain priority of religion. Kindness or love (the universal which "descends" into the particular with the design of drawing the latter up to it) is the moral duty most nearly approximating religion, in a sense, and forming the link between morality and religion.[157] This is evident in light of the fact that the obligation central to both morality and religion signifies self-sacrifice or duties to a being or beings outside the self (ultimately, to God in religion). Finally, in this regard, Harris claims that

"Moral law, as thus shown to be the foundation of civilization and all successful human endeavor, is next akin to religion."[158]

The other feature of the philosophical paradox is the *separation* of morality and religion on the basis of the separation of the secular and religious realms of life. In modern times (from Harris's perspective), there is seen the evolution of "two distinct elements, the religious and the secular, continually becoming more explicit and independent, while they develop more and more into harmony, in what they embody."[159] Therefore, one finds a kind of Hegelian dialectic: the close bond between morality and religion is torn asunder by means of the development of a separation between the two, within which arises a new type of harmony.[160]

> The secular becomes independent of the religious, not in the sense that it alone is all sufficient for man, but only in the sense that it is capable of directing its own sphere in harmony with religion, and consequently does not need interference or guidance from it. Into the realms of the secular has been transferred and recognized the religious principle of human responsibility.[161]

An example of correlative areas of responsibility is crime and sin, the former attributed to a person who breaks the "laws of Right" and the latter to one who violates the "mandate of Religion." Crime and sin correspond to one another, but they also differ radically.[162] The "Christian idea" is referred to as furnishing the exclusive foundation for the possibility of the separation of the state and religion as existing institutions.[163]

What are the meanings of this philosophical paradox relative to the relationship between morality and education? As could be anticipated, the intimate bond between morality and religion suggests the close relationship which Harris depicts among morality, religion, and education. Also, thrusting the government into the picture, he says the following about the connection ("which we see everywhere existing") between education and the national religion: "The national religion in defining its relation to God, defines its idea of the final destiny of man. Not only does education, moral and intellectual, depend directly upon this, but the form of government, the constitution of civil society, likewise presuppose that basis."[164] In other words, secular society, in general (extending somewhat the notion of constitutional government), and education, in particular, are guided directly by the idea of the final destiny of the human person suggested by religion.

The bond, however, between religion (and morality) and education is countered by an application of the separation of morality and religion in the above account. This separation provides the basis for the establishment of the principle that morality *without religion* holds a prominent place in the public school. A practical principle underlying this position is that whatever the church has nurtured to a point of maturity, allowing it to live and to thrive independently, should not continue to be supported by ecclesiastical authority. Since the code of moral duties is recognized by the state as necessary for social well-being, religion will gain by allowing the state to sponsor moral education. If the school effectively assumes responsibility for motivating the student to form character based upon self-control and self-denial without appealing to the ultimate ground of obligation found in religion, then religion discovers that its presuppositions are already developed in the mind of the youth. Morality taught in this way promotes the advancement of religion and strengthens its hold because of the "ready entrance" of religion into a community where justice resides.[165]

The following passage of Harris is worth citing as a succinct summary of his position regarding morality without religion in the public school:

> ... Public School education is moral and completely so, on its own basis; ... it lays the basis for religion, *but is not a substitute for religion*. It is not a substitute for the State because it teaches justice—it only prepares an indispensable culture for the citizen of the State. The State must exist; Religion must exist and complement the structure of human culture begun in moral education. But it is better for Religion that independent institutions—State and School—establish on a purely secular basis such discipline as the church would be under the necessity of establishing for its own preservation, were they not otherwise provided.[166]

Religion, of course, is not left without its educational implications. In fact, implicit in the above remarks is a need for religious education to complement the secularized moral education in the public school. The importance and scope of religious education is suggested in the following citation:

> The church, by having a portion of its work taken from it, will, perforce, intensify its efforts on the remaining functions. Doubtless there is infinite occasion for this concentration: for this age is justly called materialistic and stands in need of a theoretical consciousness of the Divine; its practical consciousness of the Divine is everywhere manifest in the progress of humanitarian civilization. The relation of the Human to the Divine cannot form a subject of legislation in a free state nor a topic of instruction in public schools; the church justly claims the prerogative of enlightening man on the highest of all themes.[167]

This example of Harris's philosophy of moral education is a corollary of the previous one, completing it (relatively speaking) through advertence to the relationship between morality and religion, and the impact of that relationship upon the public school. As indicated, there is a very close parallel between (on one hand) a) the theoretical bond between morality and religion,

b) the separation of the two (on the basis of the divorce of the secular and the sacred), and c) the resultant harmony between them; and (on the other hand) a) the similar kind of influence of morality and religion upon education (and the fact that religion possesses the common basis for morality and education), b) the necessity of teaching morality without religion in the public school, and c) the complementary nature of moral and religious education.

This section on Harris's moral (and religious) philosophy and its bearing upon education was introduced with a brief example relating the notions of moral virtues and vices to the basic purpose of moral education and to one specific means to that end. Some details of this framework were elaborated in the second example by analyzing the basic meaning and pre-supposition of "ethical system," and the nature of various moral obligations which centers upon self-sacrifice; and by seeking implications of these principles (according to Harris) for the purposes, agencies, and substance of moral education, within which strict discipline is all-important. The third example complements the second in that it demonstrates a parallel between the relationship of morality and religion, on one hand, and moral and religious education, on the other hand. Although Harris's view of religion in this Report is bound closely to his theory of morality, one can extract an example of philosophy of education within this last example by relating his brief comments on philosophy of religion to similarly brief observations on religious education.[168] That will be done in the following and last major section.

Religion and Education

The philosophy of religion and its relationship to religious education appears to be the most important area in Harris's philosophy of education as it is discussed in the Annual Reports. That could not be concluded from the space he attributes to it in these Reports, however. For various reasons, especially the fact that the Reports pertain to the public schools and religious education (in his view) is a responsibility of the church, he provides in the Reports only an outline of the direction of his thought on this topic. In fact, the first of two examples is extracted from the last example in the above section on morality and education. Only a sketch of it will be provided here to illustrate the relationship between the philosophy of religion and religious education.

It was noted above that in "religion," according to Harris, one locates the source of descriptions of the relationship between the human person and God; and explanations of the final destiny of the person, and of the meaning of "the ultimate and supreme ground of all obligation."[169] In a very brief passage[170] the function of religious education is ascribed (at least implicitly) to the church, which is judged to be responsible for counteracting the materialistic age. This anti-materialist stance is to be promulgated (apparently) by inculcating (through a process of religious education, it can be presumed) "a theoretical consciousness of the Divine," and, supposedly, the theory and practice of a suitable relationship of human beings to God. This relationship is referred to as "the highest of all themes,"[171] which is the prerogative of the church to teach. This position seems to make the church the supreme agency of education, and religious education the primary dimension of the whole educative process. In this example it is evident that Harris's version of religious education is entirely consistent with his conception of religion. Furthermore, from what is known about his scholarship, it can be assumed that the latter exercised a direct influence upon the former in his thought.

The second and last example of Harris's philosophy of education relative to religious matters also is extremely brief. Religion is considered in this context as a sphere of the theory of the human person,[172] "wherein man strives to elevate himself above all visible forms to the Absolute Ideal through devotion and worship."[173] Harris makes only one statement concerning education here, but it is an important one to him and a direct consequence of religion as a theory of the human person: "It [religion] is so important that it belongs to an education apart from the rest, a sacred education to be found within the Church and not side by side with other branches in secular education."[174] Therefore, it is clear that, due to the nature and importance of religion, religious education under the auspices of the church is the most important of all forms of education.

In these two brief examples of Harris's philosophy of education relative to religion and education, it is evident that religion is centered upon the relationship between the human person and God. Because this is inherently the most important of all human concerns, the church holds the proper authority for guiding persons in this realm, religious education has a very special place in the general process of human formation, and the church becomes the most significant agency of education.

Summary

The following is a brief summary of the six categories of examples of Superintendent William Torrey Harris's philosophy of education in his Annual Reports as elaborated above. The structure of philosophy of education discovered in the Annual Reports of Superintendent Harris lies in the application of philosophical principles to educational questions and topics. Although there is a dialectical interrelationship between the two major poles of this framework, the most logical approach is from the philosophical awareness to the resolution of educational issues. That is the order followed in this interpretation, which suggests that the central theme is a broadly based philosophical anthropology (or philosophy of the person) in relationship primarily to the purposes, curriculum, and teaching methods desirable in intellectual, moral, and religious education. The six philosophical categories chosen for consideration in relationship to educational matters, according to Harris, are philosophy of the person in general, philosophical psychology and epistemology, social and political philosophy, philosophy of freedom, moral philosophy, and philosophy of religion. While the exemplification of the application of philosophical principles to education does not follow precisely Harris's own order of analysis, each example is derived from the same general context of the same Report.

Six examples of Harris's philosophy of education are considered in the first section, "Nature of the person, in general, and education." The philosophical themes include the person as a potentially and actually rational being, the individual and social development of the child, the substance of human character, two versions of human development, and the final cause or essence of life. The educational areas most prominent are the purposes of education and the curriculum. Agencies of education are also mentioned, and special topics addressed are the kindergarten and ethnic education. The next five categories are derived from key characteristics of the "person, in general." Under "The human mind and education" (in which there are six examples), the philosophical keynote is the three-stage process of cognition by means of which the person transcends an awareness of physical objects in developing an appreciation of relationships and, eventually, universal truths. For education, these cognitive processes of perception, understanding, and reason suggest the necessity of the student's self-activity through all three stages, the necessity of teaching general principles based in several specific subjects, and the necessity of employing teaching methods which will avoid "arrested development." Other educational topics here are the responsibility of the educator to induce the "self-estrangement" of the student, and two levels of education. The need for co-education is based upon Harris's philosophical perspective on the male-female relationship.

The central theme of "Human socialization and education" (with eight examples) is the necessity of the individual to participate physically and spiritually with others through social organizations in order to become truly human, with implications for education. The spiritual side of combination is the more important and, therefore, holds a greater significance for the establishment of educational ideals. Specific philosophical topics include the following: the processes of physical and spiritual socialization; socialization as a process of "balancing" spontaneity and obedience; socialization as a means to genuine originality and genius; the necessity of social institutions for socialization and of the role of language for sharing universalized meaning; specific social institutions in the process of socialization; pluralistic democracy and socialization; the essence of the person as found in combination with others; and the personal struggle required for human combination. Educational matters of most concern are the typical ones: purposes, curriculum, and teaching methods (including the use of instruments such as the daily newspaper and the library).

"Human freedom and education" is focused upon four major examples in which considerations of the purposes and agencies of education, the curriculum, and teaching methods were "extracted" from an assertion of the reality of the independence of the individual person and national self-government, a view of human freedom based upon the notion of the person emphasizing the rational and social dimensions, an explanation of the two correlative aspects of freedom, and a description of freedom through self-knowledge. The fifth section, "Morality (and religion) and education" (with three examples), is centered upon the basic meaning and presupposition of "ethical system" and the nature of various moral obligations centering upon self-sacrifice, with implications for the purposes, agencies, and substance of moral education, within which strict discipline is all-important. Furthermore, the relationship between morality and religion is seen as a parallel to the relationship between moral and religious education. In the two brief examples under "Religion and education," religion is centered upon the relationship between the human person and God. Since this is inherently the most important of all human concerns, and since the church maintains the proper authority for guiding persons in this realm, religious education has a very special place in the general process of human formation, according to Harris, and the church becomes the most significant agency of education.

The importance of the interrelationships and the unity of these six categories of examples scarcely can be overemphasized in an effort to appreciate Harris's philosophy of education in his Annual Reports. Attention is given to this topic in the Summary and Conclusion.

NOTES

1. This statement, as well as the general orientation here, presumes the structure of philosophy of education to consist of distinctly philosophical principles applied (explicitly or implicitly) to educational questions or topics. While this framework can be adapted to various modes of philosophy other than Harris's idealism (for example, realism and existentialism), it fails to accommodate thoroughly some other modes (for example, instrumentalism and linguistic analysis).

2. Some evidence for this identification can be found in the general tenor of Harris's orientation; more specifically, there is his book *Psychologic Foundations of Education*, which is a basic textbook in philosophy of education.

3. Fourteenth Annual Report, 96.

4. Ibid.

5. Nineteenth Annual Report of the Board of Directors of the St. Louis Public Schools, for the Year Ending August 1, 1873 (St. Louis: Democrat Litho. and Printing Company, 1874), 72–73.

6. Eighteenth Annual Report of the Board of Directors of the St. Louis Public Schools, for the Year Ending August 1, 1872 (St. Louis: Democrat Litho. and Printing Company, 1873), 142.

7. Fourteenth Annual Report, 92.

8. Twenty-second annual Report of the Board of Directors of the St. Louis Public Schools, for the Year Ending August 1, 1876 (St. Louis: Slawson, Printer, 1877), 96.

9. Ibid., 119.

10. The relationship between religion and philosophy does not seem to be entirely clear in these Annual Reports, for one reason because it is not treated systematically or at great length. However, Harris's approach to religious matters appears to lie within the realm of philosophy of religion.

11. Seventeenth Annual Report of the Board of Directors of the St. Louis Public Schools, for the Year Ending August 31, 1871 (St. Louis: Plate, Olshausen and Company, Printers and Binders, 1872), 22–23.

12. It should be noted that no claim is made in the Annual Reports or in this interpretation that the educational implications pointed out are the only possibilities on the basis of the philosophical principles explicated. On the other hand, this does not mean that the relationship between the two sides is arbitrary or meaningless.

13. Twenty-fifth Annual Report of the Board of Directors of the St. Louis Public Schools, for the Year Ending August 1, 1879 (St. Louis: G.I. Jones and Company, Printers, 1880), 215.

14. Ibid., 205. (This point is related directly by Harris to the intellectual value of the "gifts" of Froebel, which are central to the latter's theory of kindergarten education.)

15. Ibid., 215.

16. Fifteenth Annual Report of the Board of Directors of the St. Louis Public Schools, for the Year Ending August 1, 1869. (St. Louis: Democrat Book and Job Printing House, 1870), 111.

17. Ibid., 128. See also 136 of the same report.

18. Under Harris's auspices as Superintendent, the first public school kindergarten in the United States was established in the St. Louis Public Schools in 1873.

19. Twenty-fifth Annual Report, 129.

20. Ibid.

21. Ibid., 137. (Harris's model for kindergarten education is derived primarily from Friedrich Froebel [1782–1852], a German educator.)

22. Twenty-first Annual Report of the Board of Directors of the St. Louis Public Schools, for the Year Ending August 1, 1875 (St. Louis: Globe-Democrat Job Printing Company, 1876), 113.

23. Ibid., 112–13. (Apparently, this recommendation applies to elementary and secondary schools.)
24. Twenty-fifth Annual Report, 192–94.
25. Ibid., 192–95.
26. Ibid., 221.
27. Ibid., 221.
28. Nineteenth Annual Report, 152.
29. Ibid., 153.
30. Ibid. (The school, as such, is not mentioned among these educational agencies, apparently due to the general topic, the public school library.)
31. Ibid.
32. Twenty-third Annual Report, 193. See also the Twenty-second Annual Report, 96, 119, for a similar point of view concerning Froebel.
33. Twenty-third Annual Report, 193–94. Philosophy of the curriculum is only one dimension of Harris's philosophy of mind and education, of course. Educational topics other than the curriculum also are considered, as is seen below.
34. Ibid., 227.
35. Ibid., 225, 227.
36. Nineteenth Annual Report, 186–88.
37. Ibid., 186.
38. Ibid., 186–88.
39. Fourteenth Annual Report, 90.
40. Ibid., 91.
41. Ibid.
42. Ibid., 90.
43. Ibid., 94.
44. Ibid.
45. Ibid., 95.
46. Nineteenth Annual Report, 63–65.
47. Plato, *The Republic*, Book VII.
48. Nineteenth Annual Report, 63–65.
49. Twenty-fifth Annual Report, 211.
50. Ibid. (In an analogy, Harris likens the smoke and flame to instinct and national purpose.)
51. Ibid., 212. See also 211.
52. Ibid., 212. (Although Harris does not make explicit in this passage the connection between the moral habits and intellection, elsewhere he comments on the relationship between intellect and will; at any rate, the link is quite evident.)
53. Ibid., 198–200.
54. Nineteenth Annual Report, 108.
55. Ibid., 117.
56. Ibid., 106–20. Harris distinguishes between these two features, claiming that "The demand for the same course of study is paramount, that for co-education subordinate, although of considerable importance" (120).
57. Fifteenth Annual Report, 109.

58. Ibid., 109–10.
59. Ibid., 110.
60. Ibid.
61. Ibid. See, also, the Sixteenth Annual Report of the Board of Directors of the St. Louis Public Schools, for the year ending August 1, 1870 (St. Louis: [s.n.], 1871), 175, for the importance and the purpose of the school in regard to socialization.
62. The following classification of the Public School Library seems to indicate Harris's view of the division of knowledge:
I. Philosophy (Science of Sciences)
II. Theology (Science of God)
III. Social and Political Sciences (treating of human institutions: state, society, and language), whose subdivisions are
   1) Jurisprudence
   2) Politics
   3) Social Science
   4) Philology
IV. Natural Sciences and Useful Arts (Nature and its uses), subdivided into
   1) Mathematics (treating of the pure form of Nature)
   2) Physics
   3) Natural History
   4) Medicine
   5) Useful Arts
Ibid., 111.
63. Ibid., 111–15. (The cited phrase is on 115.)
64. Ibid., 113.
65. Twenty-fourth Annual Report of the Board of Directors of the St. Louis Public Schools, for the Year Ending August 1, 1878 (St. Louis: Max Olshausen, Printers, 1879), 201.
66. Ibid.
67. Ibid., 201–02. (The citation is from 202).
68. Twenty-second Annual Report, 186–87.
69. Ibid., 187.
70. Ibid.
71. Ibid., 186.
72. The "older" methods of teaching referred to by Harris are the oral method and the textbook method. The "newer" method is called "independent experiment" or "original investigation." Ibid., 184–86.
73. Ibid., 186–87. (The citation is from 187.)
74. Ibid., 141.
75. Ibid., 137.
76. Ibid., 138.
77. Ibid., 137.
78. Ibid.
79. Twenty-fifth Annual Report, 227.
80. Ibid., 227–28.

81. Ibid., 228.
82. Ibid.
83. Ibid., 229–30.
84. Twenty-first Annual Report, 111–12.
85. Ibid., 112–13.
86. Ibid., 111.
87. Ibid., 112.
88. Ibid.
89. Nineteenth Annual Report, 152.
90. Ibid., 152–53.
91. Ibid., 153.
92. Ibid.
93. Ibid. The major points of this example regarding spiritual communion and the means to it also are discussed in the Twenty-fifth Annual Report, 217–18. There, Harris notes that the individual, as such, can become "generic," that is, "realize in himself the rationality of the entire species of the human race" by means of the "instrumentalities of intercommunication." Most of the instrumentalities named here (as the scientific society, the publishing house, the bookstore, the library, the school, and the newspaper) are, in themselves, directly educative. At any rate, one of the purposes of education is "to give to the individual the means of this participation in the aggregate labors of all humanity." Specific means which can be employed by the individual to attain the ideal are the institutions of family, civil society (including schools), the state, and the church.
94. Twenty-third Annual Report, 195.
95. Ibid.
96. Fifteenth Annual Report, 27.
97. Ibid.
98. Ibid.
99. Twenty-fifth Annual Report, 215–16. (The quotation is from 216).
100. Ibid., 219.
101. Twenty-fifth Annual Report, 217.
102. Ibid., 213.
103. Not all self-activity is impulse or instinct, according to Harris. He also uses the terms to signify a more positive response of the person, as such.
104. Twenty-fifth Annual Report, 218.
105. Ibid.
106. Ibid.
107. Ibid., 219. Harris attributes to Froebel's method of instruction "the preservation of the *form* of play, and at the same time the introduction of the *substance* of prescription."
108. Sixteenth Annual Report, 178.
109. Ibid.
110. Ibid., 179.
111. Ibid. This notion is elaborated somewhat in the Twenty-second Annual Report, 107–08, where he refers to "the process of converting a free activity, a new

thought, into an unconscious habit [which] is, after all, the process of freeing the will and the intellect from its concentration on a lower activity, in order that it may energize anew upon a larger synthesis."

112. Sixteenth Annual Report, 180.
113. Ibid., 181.
114. Ibid., 175, 176.
115. Ibid., 176.
116. The need for promoting the student's initiative to think new thoughts and yet to render thinking habitual by repetition without making it dull is considered by Harris in the Twenty-second Annual Report, 207–08.
117. Sixteenth Annual Report, 176–77.
118. Twenty-second Annual Report, 193.
119. Although Harris focuses on the material fruits of combination here, the spiritual benefits are the more lasting and important, as has been seen above.
120. Twenty-second Annual Report, 194.
121. Nineteenth Annual Report, 68.
122. bid.
123. bid., 69.
124. Ibid.
125. Ibid., 71.
126. Ibid.
127. The relationship of religion to the school is discussed below.
128. Nineteenth Annual Report, 71. (In the same Annual Report, on 73, Harris attributes to the study of Latin a "subtle, spiritual gain derived from the increase of mental strength to analyze and combine the elements of human interests. . . .")
129. Sixteenth Annual Report, 23.
130. bid.
131. Seventeenth Annual Report, 21.
132. Ibid., 35.
133. Ibid., 28–29.
134. Ibid., 29–30.
135. Ibid., 30.
136. Ibid., 30–31.
137. Ibid., 26.
138. Ibid., 80. The remaining remarks concerning moral education are directed exclusively, or nearly so, to the school.
139. Ibid., 21. (Moral education is complementary to intellectual education, "the discipline and instruction of the intellect.")
140. Ibid., 76.
141. Ibid., 77.
142. Ibid., 78.
143. Ibid., 31–35.
144. Ibid., 31.
145. Ibid., 32.
146. Ibid., 33.

147. Ibid., 34.
148. Ibid.
149. Ibid., 35.
150. Ibid., 35–36.
151. Ibid., 36.
152. Ibid., 80.
153. Ibid., 81.
154. Ibid., 83–84.
155. Ibid., 22–23. The definitions referred to are interpretations based on what Harris says in this passage concerning "national religion."
156. Ibid., 26.
157. Ibid., 30–31.
158. Ibid., 27.
159. Ibid., 24.
160. This appears to be a prime instance of Harris's use of the Hegelian dialectic of thesis, antithesis, and synthesis.
161. Seventeenth Annual Report, 25.
162. Ibid.
163. Ibid., 24.
164. Ibid., 23.
165. Ibid., 27.
166. Ibid., 36–37.
167. Ibid., 37.
168. In the Eighteenth Annual Report, 16–17, Harris provides a brief summary of some of these principles of morality and moral education in relationship to religious considerations.
169. Seventeenth Annual Report, 22–23. See also 49.
170. Ibid., 52.
171. Ibid., 37.
172. This is the fourth sphere mentioned, and it is addressed parenthetically. The first three spheres, in order, are man as a practical being, man as a theoretical being, and man as an artist. Nineteenth Annual Report, 75.
173. Ibid.
174. Ibid.

Chapter Three

Summary and Conclusion

The Annual Reports of the Board of Directors of the St. Louis Public Schools at one time were intended to be descriptive educational documents. These include, of course, those particular Reports compiled under the Superintendency of William Torrey Harris from 1868 to 1880. While no one could claim reasonably that Harris's Annual Reports are not educational documents, it appears that they are much more than that. Evidence for this assertion lies in the fact that Harris produced in his Annual Reports a network of philosophical principles which he employed as a substratum for the elaboration of his educational theory. Not only does Harris write about philosophy of education (stressing its importance) in his Annual Reports, but also he does philosophy of education. While the relationships between his philosophical reflections and his educational principles in these Reports are not explicated as systematically as they might have been, the content provided allows for the construction of examples of his philosophy of education based exclusively on the texts.[1]

The substance of the examples of Harris's philosophy of education which is analyzed in this book is focused upon a broadly based philosophical anthropology (or philosophy of the person) in relationship primarily to the purposes, curriculum, and teaching methods desired in intellectual, moral, and religious education. The first category of examples centers upon Harris's philosophy of the person, in general, and its implications for education, while the next five sections are classified according to key philosophical attributes of the person: mindfulness, socialization, freedom, morality, and religiousness. These five characteristics are featured (in order) in Harris's philosophical psychology and epistemology, social and political philosophy, philosophy of freedom, moral philosophy, and philosophy of religion. In each section, the philosophical principles are related to educational topics by means of two or more examples.

As stated above, the importance of the interrelationships and the unity of these six categories scarcely can be overemphasized in any attempt to appreciate Harris's philosophy of education in his Annual Reports. Some basic features of these interrelationships and this unity can be synthesized by adverting to his dualistic conception of the person and the consequent educational purposes; these features characterize the general spirit of the philosophy of education which emerges from the six categories of examples. The dualistic conception of the human being is based upon the fundamental distinction between matter and spirit, which is humanly manifested in the body and soul. The powers of the soul consist of the intellect (for knowing) and the will (for choosing). This material-spiritual being called the human person also can be viewed as individual or social. Only through socialization, or combination with others in physical and spiritual manners, can authentic humanization in relationship with God occur. Within this dualistic framework, the immaterial is afforded a primacy which is extremely significant for the purposes of education.

Education, in implementing the development of the person, must take serious account of this dualistic structure of reality. Its purposes include developing the body and the soul, including the intellect and the will, in a manner conducive to physical and spiritual combination with others, which makes human persons truly free beings. In all cases, the physical growth is intended generally to serve and to promote spiritual maturation. The latter when attached to the intellect is intellectual education; when associated with the will, it is moral education; and when it is directed to the union of the person with the Divine, it is religious education. Intellectual education is established upon a curriculum with five subjects of study, which is gradually expanded as the student enters the higher levels of the process. Moral education is undertaken with a basic intent to discipline the student in order to promote an attitude of self-sacrifice. Religious education is the highest form of education and is to be conducted under the auspices of the church.

The philosophical principles proposed are consistent with—and quite certainly inspired—the pattern of education recommended. A basic example of this consistency lies in the parallel between different modes of being (intellect, will, and God) and different kinds of education (intellectual, moral, and religious).[2]

This investigation into Harris's philosophy of education in the Annual Reports suggests several vital areas for further study. First of all, in light of the present state of pertinent research, one can still wonder legitimately about detailed evidence concerning the relative completeness or fullness of the development of Harris's philosophy of education in the Annual Reports in relationship to his later writings.[3] Another topic of historical interest is a comparison of his Annual Reports compiled for the St. Louis Public Schools

Summary and Conclusion

with those he presented to the Board of Education in Concord, Massachusetts, while he was serving as Superintendent of the Concord Public Schools from 1882 to 1885. A third topic for detailed scrutiny is the bearing of his philosophy of education upon his practical decisions as a school superintendent in St. Louis and in Concord.

Fourthly, while many presume that Harris is a strict follower of Hegel, not all commentators concur in that opinion. A part of the same consideration is the opposition between those who claim that Harris is an *absolute* idealist and others who contend that he is a *personal* idealist.[4] Intimately related to this last item, fifthly, is the question of Harris' originality as a philosopher (of education). As far as his philosophy, as such, is concerned, the common view seems to be that, although he was not an original thinker, he rendered major contributions to American philosophy through founding and editing the *Journal of Speculative Philosophy*, the first American journal devoted exclusively to philosophy, and through the founding of the St. Louis Philosophical Society.[5] Furthermore, he is given credit for a certain kind of originality in his pioneering efforts to relate his philosophical idealism to educational problems.[6] In fact, he has been referred to as "the first native American philosopher of education."[7]

Sixthly, an area for further inquiry is suggested by references to Harris's contributions to American philosophy and philosophy of education.[8] What was his role and place in American philosophy of education? He is said to have wielded an extraordinary influence[9] (in philosophy and in education) during his lifetime, but why did that influence diminish so abruptly? What caused the sudden demise of his popularity in American intellectual circles?[10] These questions touch upon the relationship of Harris's philosophy of education to the intellectual-cultural revolution occurring in the United States between 1880 and 1920. The "watershed" of the 1890s was followed by the twentieth-century reactions of the pragmatists, realists, and naturalists to various forms of idealism.[11] These three movements tended to be "replaced" in twentieth-century American philosophy and philosophy of education by analytic philosophies, whose general effect has been to narrow the scope of philosophy of education; to prescribe a more technical language; to divorce philosophy of education from theological considerations; and to diminish widespread communication among philosophers of education, and between philosophers of education and educators in general.[12] These recent and contemporary trends in American philosophy and philosophy of education raise questions of the pertinence and importance of Harris's philosophy of education for the present. Is it worthy of our attention today?

In conclusion, while the primary sources utilized in this paper were intended officially to be descriptions of the process of education (in the St. Louis

Public Schools), it is evident that William Torrey Harris produced in them a network of philosophical principles elaborated in relationship to, and as a foundation for, his educational theory. The interpretation of his thought provided in this book illustrates a structure of philosophy of education which is not only still viable, but also necessary.

NOTES

1. The important point regarding the textual base is that neither side of the relationship (philosophy or education) needs to be supplied by the interpreter in order to present a philosophy of education.

2. The physical being of the person is involved, of course, in all three kinds of education. It is prominent in a special manner in moral education, where the person is to be moved to undertake certain physical acts (as, for example, in the student's duty to be punctual).

3. An important source to be utilized in this regard is Harris's only full-length book on philosophy of education, *Psychologic Foundations of Education: An Attempt to Show the Genesis of the Higher Faculties of the Mind*, 1898.

4. Two sources of discussions of absolute and personal idealism are the following: John Macquarrie, *Twentieth-century Religious Thought: The Frontiers of Philosophy and Theology, 1900–1970*, Revised edition (London: SCM Press, Ltd., 1971), Chapters II and III; and James E. Creighton, *Studies in Speculative Philosophy* (New York: The Macmillan Company, 1925; New York: Kraus Reprint Co., 1970), Chapter XIV.

5. See Leidecker, 316, 314–27. *The Journal of Speculative Philosophy* is characterized here as "America's first serial publication of a professional philosophic nature" (324). (Its contributors included William James, Josiah Royce, Charles Pierce, John Dewey, Thomas Davidson, G. Stanley Hall, G.H. Howison, and Nicholas Murray Butler.) Along with the *JSP*, the St. Louis Philosophical Society was "instrumental in bringing about one of the most significant movements in the history of American philosophy, the St. Louis Movement in Philosophy. . . ." (316).

6. See Roberts, "Educational Contributions of William Torrey Harris," *Studies in Honor of William Torrey Harris, International Education Review*, 37. According to Roberts, Harris "was a profound philosopher who put his theories, tested in the light of eternal principles, into school practice and at the same time examined all pedagogic principles by means of his mature metaphysical tenets" (237).

7. I have not been able to re-locate this citation. However, certainly, one of the most pertinent sources is J.J. Chambliss, *The Origins of American Philosophy of Education: Its Development as a Distinct Discipline, 1808–1913* (The Hague, Netherlands: Martinus Nijhoff, 1968).

8. While countless pages of print have been produced to explicate the history of American philosophy, the history of American philosophy of education has yet to be published. However, from the primary sources commonly known, there is reason to

suggest that the latter closely parallels the former in regard to the general development of philosophical schools and movements.

9. For example, see Butler, "Foreword", Leidecker, *Yankee Teacher*, 4; Curti, 310; Monroe (ed.), *The Cyclopedia of Education*, Vol. III, 220; and Kilpatrick, "Tendencies in Educational Philosophy," *Twenty-five Years of American Education*, Ed. Kandel, 61.

10. See Kilpatrick, "Tendencies in Educational Philosophy," *Twenty-five Years of American Education*, Ed. Kandel, for the question.

11. For example, see Commager, *The American Mind: An Interpretation of American Thought and Character Since the 1880s*.

12. The fact of a thorough indifference to philosophy of education (in any technical use of the term) in official statements of several large city public school systems and state departments of education in the United States is clearly evident from the unpublished results of a survey taken during the fall of 1979.

The fact that philosophers of education are not habitually addressing the kinds of issues which attract the attention of educators, in general, was strongly suggested by the Dean of the School of Education at Stanford University in his welcome address at the Annual Meeting of the Philosophy of Education Society in San Francisco on April 27, 1980. On that occasion he made the following three comments.

"1) It is not clear that philosophers of education are addressing some of the major moral and social issues in education (such as the growth of private schools or the practice of using children as primary agents in addressing some of the Nations most vexing social problems).

2) Much of the writing by educational philosophers seems directed toward other educational philosophers. As in much humanistically oriented scholarship these days, expository styles tend to be opaque. Educational philosophers would do well to cultivate literary approaches that are at once valued by academic scholars and also by those who have most to gain by a greater understanding of the philosophical basis for education policy.

3) Some education philosophers use their scholarship primarily to advance their own political preferences. While there is no particular objection to this development, most people who have responsibilities for teaching or school administration would just as soon trust their own political judgment as someone else's. If education philosophy is seen as partisan in a narrowing sense, it is taken less seriously." (These remarks are cited from a letter addressed to me by Myron C. Atkin, in which, at my request, he summarized the main points of his address.)

Finally, in this regard, it appears not unlikely that existential connections could be ascertained among the following: 1) the indifference to philosophy of education exhibited in certain official statements of large city public school systems and state departments of education, 2) the failure of philosophers of education to address various questions prominent in the history of philosophy (of education), 3) the prevalence of analytic philosophies in American philosophy and philosophy of education, and 4) the dearth of teaching positions in philosophy of education in the United States.

Chapter Four

Epilogue

What is the significance of William Torrey Harris for American philosophy and education in the twentieth century? Judging by the pertinent literature since 1920, eleven years after his death, one answer is quite clear: very little! However, I am among those (if, in fact, there are others) who contend that his writings are highly important, not only for appreciating the meaning and direction of where we have been, but where we ought to be going.

The historical development of twentieth-century philosophy and education in the United States cannot be traced meaningfully without some attention to the intellectual-cultural revolution between 1880 and 1920. In the realm of philosophy, the shift in emphases has been described as follows: from natures and essences to phenomena and appearances; from permanence to constant change; from belief in a Transcendent Being to exclusive reliance upon the human and natural—in general, from various types of idealism to diverse formulations of naturalism and pragmatism. In the arena of education, the transition has been catalogued as follows: from goals based upon permanent, transcendent realities and stable, terrestrial norms to constantly changing circumstances; from a curriculum of subject matter set out in advance to be mastered by students to a curriculum of information based upon the perceived needs of students; from teaching students how to think abstractly and concretely to promoting students how to use data in relating satisfactorily to the environment; from an emphasis upon listening and discussing to learning by living—in general, from so-called traditional education to progressive or "new" education.

The history of philosophy of American education has never been published, and, to my knowledge, there are no noteworthy historical analyses of philosophy of education covering this revolutionary period (1880–1920). However, the 1890s has been referred to as the "watershed" of American intellectual history, and the period from 1893 to 1918 has been called "twenty-five years of educational revolution." The latter dates designate the promulgation of two landmark reports of the National Education Association focusing on secondary education: the Committee of Ten Report (1893) and the *Cardinal Principles of Secondary Education* (1918). William Torrey Harris, as US Commissioner of Education, was a member of the Committee of Ten and penned its Letter of Transmittal. His educational theory can be related favorably to the proposal of the Committee of Ten, the first nationally organized group to report on American education. While the 1893 report (as the 1918 document) was devoid of any explicit philosophical content, Harris's philosophical principles bear a very meaningful relationship to the Committee of Ten's educational plan.

Attention to this revolutionary period represents a potential initiation of any attempt to answer the question of Harris's relationship to twentieth-century American philosophy, education, and philosophy of education. The remainder of the story centers upon mainstream philosophical developments in naturalism, pragmatism, linguistic philosophies, and postmodernism. In education, while progressive education (featuring the comprehensive high school and differentiated curriculum) received substantial criticism (especially in the 1950s and in the 1980s), it by and large carried the day from 1920 to the end of the twentieth century and into the twenty-first. Proper attention to these topics and to their interrelationships, I contend, would provide a context for a positive view and promise of the philosophy of education of William Torrey Harris today, especially concerning 1) the openness to transcendence in his philosophical questioning, and 2) the manner in which he employs philosophical principles to provide meaning and justification for his pedagogical theory.

In my judgment, these two features of Harris's philosophy of education are extremely significant for three reasons. 1) A Transcendent Reality does exist as the beacon of our lives. 2) As Jacques Maritain claims in *Education at the Crossroads* (1943), every educational creed bears the stamp of philosophical principles—recognized or not. 3) If anything stands out in the literature on the history of American education from about 1950 to 2000, it is the practically total neglect of any consideration of kinds of philosophy potentially capable of suitably guiding educational planning. This neglect in our culture has contributed immeasurably to public indifference to philosophy, inattention to fundamental human values, miscommunication, misinterpretation, contradiction, and just simply ineffective education. While Harris offers no panacea for the ill effects of recent and present American philosophy and education, attention to his thought could initiate a desperately needed renewal.

Bibliography

ANNUAL REPORTS OF THE BOARD OF DIRECTORS OF THE ST. LOUIS PUBLIC SCHOOLS

Thirteenth Annual Report for the Year Ending August 1, 1867. St. Louis: Missouri Democrat Book and Job Printing House, 1867.
Fourteenth Annual Report for the Year Ending August 1, 1868. St. Louis: George Knapp and Company, Printers and Binders, 1869.
Fifteenth Annual Report for the Year Ending August 1, 1869. St. Louis: Democrat Book and Job Printing House, 1870.
Sixteenth Annual Report for the Year Ending August 1, 1870. St. Louis: [s.n.], 1871.
Seventeenth Annual Report for the Year Ending August 1, 1871. St. Louis: Plate, Olshausen and company, Printers and Binders, 1872.
Eighteenth Annual Report for the Year Ending August 1, 1872. St. Louis: Democrat Litho. and Printing Company, 1873.
Nineteenth Annual Report for the Year Ending August 1, 1873. St. Louis: Democrat Litho. and Printing Company, 1874.
Twenty-first Annual Report for the Year Ending August 1, 1875. St. Louis: Globe-Democrat Job Printing Company, 1876.
Twenty-second Annual Report for the Year Ending August 1, 1876. St. Louis: Slawson, Printer, 1877.
Twenty-third Annual Report for the Year Ending August 1, 1877. St. Louis: John J. Daly and Company, Printers, 1878.
Twenty-fourth Annual Report for the Year Ending August 1, 1878. St. Louis: Max Olshousen, 1879.
Twenty-fifth Annual Report for the Year Ending August 1, 1879. St. Louis: G.I. Jones and Company, 1880.

BOOKS

The American Hegelians: An Intellectual Episode in the History of Western America. Ed. William H. Goetzmann. New York: Alfred A. Knopf, Publisher, 1973.

Arscott, John R. *Moral Freedom and the Educative Process: A Study in the Educational Philosophy of William Torrey Harris.* New York: New York University Press, 1948.

Butler, Nicholas Murray (ed.). *Education in the United States*, A Series of Monographs. Vol. I. Albany, NY: J.B. Lyon, 1900.

Byerly, Carl Lester. *Contributions of William Torrey Harris to Public School Administration.* Chicago, IL: [s.n.], 1946.

Chambliss, J.J. *The Origins of American Philosophy of Education: Its Development as a Distinct Discipline, 1808–1913.* The Hague, Netherlands: Martinus Nijhoff, 1968.

Commager, Henry Steele. *The American Mind: An Interpretation of American Thought and Character Since the 1800s.* New Haven: Yale University Press, 1956.

Creighton, James E. *Studies in Speculative Philosophy.* New York: The Macmillan Company, 1925; New York: Kraus Reprint Company, 1970.

Curti, Merle. *The Social Ideas of American Educators.* New and revised edition. Totowa, NJ: Littlefield, Adams, 1966.

Easton, Lloyd David. *Harris, William Torrey.* [S.l.:s.n.], 1967.

Evans, Henry R. "A List of the Writings of W.T. Harris." A chapter from the *Report of the U.S. Commissioner of Education for 1906–07.* Washington, DC: Government Printing Office, 1908.

Harmon, Frances. *The Social Philosophy of the St. Louis Hegelians.* New York: [s.n.], 1943.

Harris, William Torrey. *Psychologic Foundations of Education: An Attempt to Show the Genesis of the Higher Faculties of the Mind.* International Education Series, Vol. 37. New York: D. Appleton and Company, 1898.

John, Walton C. (ed.). *William Torrey Harris: The Commemoration of the One Hundredth Anniversary of His Birth, 1835–1935.* Bulletin No. 17, Office of Education, US Department of the Interior. Washington, DC: US Government Printing Office, 1937.

Kandel, I.L. (ed.). *Twenty-five Years of American Education, Collected Essays.* New York: The Macmillan Company, 1929.

Kinzer, John Ross. *A Study of the Educational Philosophy of William Torrey Harris with Reference to the Education of Teachers.* Nashville, TN: George Peabody College for Teachers, 1940.

Kwon, Teck-Young. *A Bronson Alcott's Literary Apprenticeship to Emerson: The Role of Harris's "Journal of Speculative Philosophy."* Ann Arbor, MI: University Microfilms International, 1980.

Leidecker, Kurt F. *Yankee Teacher: The Life of William Torrey Harris.* New York: The Philosophical Library, 1946; New York: Kraus Reprint Company, 1971.

Macquarrie, John. *Twentieth-century Religious Thought: The Frontiers of Philosophy and Theology, 1900–1970.* Revised edition. London: SCM Press, Ltd., 1971.

McCluskey, Neil G. *Public Schools and Moral Educations: The Influence of Horace Mann, William Torrey Harris, and John Dewey.* New York: Columbia University Press, 1958; Westport, CT: Greenwood Press, 1975.

Monroe, Paul (ed.). *Cyclopedia of Education.* New York: the Macmillan Company, 1911–13.

Pochmann, Henry A. *New England Transcendentalism and St. Louis Hegelianism: Phases in the History of American Idealism.* New York: Haskell House, 1970 [1948].

Roberts, John S. *William Torrey Harris: A Critical Study of His Educational and Related Philosophical Views.* Washington, DC: National Education Association of the United States, 1924.

Rosenkranz, Johann K.F. *The Philosophy of Education.* International Education Series. Trans. Anna C. Brackett. New York: D. Appleton and Company, 1986.

Snider, Denton. *The St. Louis Movement in Philosophy, Literature, Education, Psychology.* St. Louis: Sigma Publishing Company, 1920.

Sniegoski, Stephen J. *William Torrey Harris and the Academic School.* Washington, DC: Department of Education, 1990.

Studies in Honor of William Torrey Harris, International Education Review. Berlin: Weidmannsche Buchhandklung, 1935.

Watson, David John. *Idealism and Social Theory: A Comparative Study of British and American Adaptations of Hegel, 1860–1914.* Philadelphia, PA: University of Pennsylvania Press, 1975.

ARTICLES

Bates, Ernest Sutherland. "Harris, William Torrey (September 10, 1835–November 5, 1909)," *Dictionary of American Biography*, (Under the Auspices of the American Council of Learned Societies), Ed. Dumas Malone. Vol.VIII. New York: Charles Scribner's Sons, 1932), 328–30.

Bennion, John W. "The School Superintendent as Philosopher," *School and Society*, 98 (January, 1970), 25–27.

Button, Henry W. "Committee of Fifteen," *History of Education Quarterly*, 5 (1965). 253–63.

Chambliss, J.J. "The Origins of History of Education in the United States: A Study of Its Nature and Purpose," *Paedagogica Historica*, 19 (1979), 94–131.

Elton, William. "Peirce's Marginalia in W.T. Harris' *Hegel's Logic, Journal of the History of Philosophy,*" 2 (1964), 82–84.

Good, James A. "A 'World-historical Idea: The St. Louis Hegelians and the Civil War," *Journal of American Studies,* 34 (December, 2000), 447–464.

"Harris, William Torrey," *Encyclopedia of the History of Missouri: A Compendium of History and Biography for Ready Reference.* Ed. Howard L. Conard. Vol.3. New York: The Southern History Company; Haldeman, Conard and Company, Proprietors, 1901), 190–201.

Sakas, Joseph. "William Torrey Harris: Pioneer in Comparative Education," *School and Society*, 99 (April, 1971), 230–32.

Troen, Selwyn. "Operation Headstart: The Beginnings of the Public School Kindergarten Movement," *Missouri Historical Review*, 66 (1972), 211–229.

Witter, Charles E. "The St. Louis Philosophical Movement and the St. Louis Public Schools," *School and Society*, 47 (March 26, 1938), 403–06.

DOCTORAL DISSERTATIONS

Kohlbrenner, Bernard J. "William Torrey Harris, Superintendent of Schools, St. Louis, Missouri, 1868–1880," Graduate School of Education, Harvard University, Cambridge, MA, 1950.

Kinser, John Ross. "A Study of the Educational Philosophy of William Torrey Harris," Peabody College for Teachers of Vanderbilt University, Nashville, TN, 1941.

Lyons, Richard G. "The Influence of Hegel on the Philosophy of Education of William Torrey Harris," Graduate School, Boston University, Boston, MA, 1964.

Nazeri, Janet Foster. "Views of Leading American Educators concerning the Schooling of Immigrant Children," College of Education, Northern Illinois University at Edwardsville, Edwardsville, IL, 1981.

MASTERS THESES

Hulan, Ruby May. "Educational Ideas of William Torrey Harris and His Contributions to American Education," Southern Methodist University, Dallas, TX, 1948.

McHatton, James. "William Torrey Harris' Theories of the Curricular Value of Natural Science," Department of Education, Northern Illinois University, Dekalb, IL, 1964.

About the Author

The teaching and research career of the author has been focused upon philosophy and education. He has taught undergraduate and graduate students in schools and departments of philosophy, and in schools and departments of education. Most of his career has been spent at Marquette University in Milwaukee, Wisconsin, but he also has taught in other universities in the United States (including the island of Guam), Australia, the Philippines, Thailand, and Taiwan. His articles in philosophy and education have appeared in about thirty different scholarly journals published in the United States, Australia, England, Ireland, India and the Philippines. He currently is a Senior Research Fellow at the Institute for the History of Philosophy and Pedagogy in Silver Spring, Maryland.

www.ingramcontent.com/pod-product-compliance
Lightning Source LLC
Chambersburg PA
CBHW032007220426
43664CB00005B/168